The Art of
SELLING TO
THE AFFLUENT

The Art of
SELLING TO THE AFFLUENT

How to Attract, Service, and Retain Wealthy Customers & Clients for Life

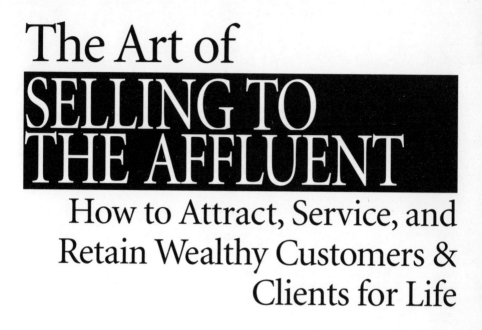

MATT OECHSLI

WILEY

JOHN WILEY & SONS, INC.

Published by John Wiley & Sons, Inc., Hoboken, New Jersey.
Published simultaneously in Canada.

For general information on our other products and services please contact our Customer Care Department within the United States at (800) 762-2974, outside the United States at (317) 572-3993 or fax (317) 572-4002.

Wiley also publishes its books in a variety of electronic formats. Some content that appears in print may not be available in electronic books. For more information about Wiley products, visit our web site at www.wiley.com.

Library of Congress Cataloging-in-Publication Data:

Oechsli, Matt.
  The art of selling to the affluent : how to attract, service, and retain wealthy customers & clients for life / Matt Oechsli.
      p.   cm.
  ISBN 0-471-70323-0 (cloth)
  1. Selling.   2. Sales presentations.   3. Affluent consumers.   I. Title.
   HF5438.25.O33   2005
   658.85—dc22
   2004017101

Printed in the United States of America.

10   9   8   7   6   5   4

CONTENTS

PREFACE

This book is about being affluent. You will immerse yourself in the world of wealth to better understand how the affluent think and act, and you will uncover the critical factors that shape their buying decisions. Everything is substantiated by research, so you can be confident of its accuracy.

Above all, this is a book about selling to the affluent. You will learn step-by-step what it takes to place yourself in the path of the affluent and effectively influence the critical factors that shape their buying decisions.

Along the way, you will also realize that this is a book about becoming affluent. You will begin to see how this approach to selling to the affluent will build your path to becoming affluent in your own right. Make that your goal, and everything you learn here will take on a whole new purpose.

Many books on selling couch old ideas under new labels and then try to make them sound fresh through the author's personal experiences. In this book, the ideas presented are new and fresh because selling to the affluent requires them to be. Those who successfully sell to the affluent quickly discover that old ideas, regardless of what they are called, more often than not, do not work.

There can be no guesswork for a salesperson committed to success in selling to the affluent. What's needed is a comprehensive how-to approach, and that's what this book provides. You will discover:

- The incredible opportunity that selling to the affluent offers.
- How the affluent think and, especially, how they make major purchase decisions.
- Ways to create the right affluent sales environment for the products and services you offer.
- How to put aside any fears you may have about approaching the affluent.
- Strategies for becoming one with the affluent and building the kind of relationships that make you magnetic.
- How to use the Internet to effectively place yourself in the path of the affluent prospects you want to attract.
- How you can provide Ritz-Carlton service with FedEx efficiency to your affluent clientele and ensure that they will keep coming back.
- How using all of the preceding information will enable you to acquire personal affluence.

We can claim that the ideas presented in this book are new and fresh for two important reasons. First, everything here is research based, and you will see evidence of that throughout. For the past five years, we have invested thousands of hours (and dollars) in studying the affluent. They have become our laboratory project. We have crawled into the mind of the affluent to take snapshot after snapshot of how they think. We have studied their perceptions and biases. Most important, we have up-to-date statistical evidence that tells us what they value when they make financial, normal budget, and major purchase buying decisions. Our most recent research was completed in June 2004, but we did not rely exclusively on our own research projects. We have also pored over every other bit of research we could find.

Second, in addition to all of this academic work, we have spent countless hours training and coaching salespeople to successfully attract, sell, service, and retain affluent customers and clients.

Everything we present in this book is research based, action oriented, and street tested.

Our objective is to provide you with a book that can serve as a current road map, guiding you to ongoing success as a salesperson who specializes in targeting the affluent. Make no mistake about it; the process described here is also designed to lead you to affluence. Make that your goal, and you will achieve even greater success than you ever imagined.

MATT OECHSLI

ACKNOWLEDGMENTS

Although there is only one name on the cover of this book, it was truly a team effort. The talents of a number of people were essential in order to make this book a reality. I would first like to thank Mike McGervey, director of training and development at the Oechsli Institute. He was the driving force behind our 2004 Affluent Major Purchase Decision Research project, and without his analytical skills I would still be interpreting all of the data. Mike was also my collaborator in writing and rewriting, and he kept me on track of what I could and could not say about our research.

As our editor, proofreader, and sanity force, Sharon Eagan has spent countless hours straining her eyes, correcting our verbiage, and referencing *The Chicago Manual of Style* and good old *Webster's Dictionary* to make certain we were communicating in a way that would be understandable to the reader. She also served to keep us sane when Mike and I would get lost in all the data from our research.

I would also like to give special thanks to Matt Holt, my editor at John Wiley & Sons, Inc., who not only identified the potential for this undertaking, but also provided the necessary guidance and patience as we worked to combine a comprehensive research project with writing a meaningful book.

The Art of
SELLING TO
THE AFFLUENT

1

THE AFFLUENT OPPORTUNITY

The prime age of the affluent consumer is between 35 and 64 years.
—Factoid, 2004 Affluent Purchasing
Decision (APD) Research*

Your future is now! Never before has there been such an opportunity to acquire personal affluence by serving the affluent. In years past, people who served wealthy people were just that—servants of those who had money and status. But times have changed. People are making more money. Those who are making more money are spending more money. Those who understand how to work with people who have money are quickly becoming affluent themselves.

Consider this book a vehicle that will enable you to travel along parallel paths. One path will take you into the heart and soul of the affluent and help you refine and ultimately master your affluent sales skills. The other path will lead you into the heart and soul of your personal dreams and aspirations and help you become affluent. As you will soon discover, these parallel paths work in concert. You will not be able to travel very far down one path without venturing an equal distance down the other. Without a personal commitment to maximize your potential in selling your products or services to the affluent, it is unlikely you will make the effort to master the art of selling to the affluent. Similarly, you will never acquire affluence by means of your sales skills without mastering the skills presented in these chapters.

---

*APD Research refers to the June 2004 research project, *How the Affluent Make Purchasing Decisions,* commissioned by the Oechsli Institute. A *factoid* is a brief fact taken from that research.

Who are the *affluent?* That's the billion-dollar question these days. The answer given is often based on what is being sold. Your neighbor who leases a new Lexus every 36 months or so would certainly fit the Lexus dealer's definition of affluent. Yet, this same neighbor might not have enough liquid assets to be pursued as an affluent prospect by a financial planner, who is more interested in the small business owner down the street who has accumulated over $1 million in investable assets, despite the fact that he or she is driving an older model vehicle.

It is immediately apparent that two totally different ways of measuring affluence are at work here:

1. *Investable assets:* The measure of affluence that the financial services industry wants to know. The financial advisor (salesperson) is trying to calculate the prospective client's risk tolerance to determine how to balance protecting those assets over the long term with getting the highest possible investment return over the next 12 months or so.

2. *Household income:* The measure of affluence that drives most major purchases. The salesperson is trying to figure out what it will take to satisfy the prospective customer's present needs and wants, how much the customer will pay to be satisfied today, and what it will take to retain that customer for the near future.

Much of the research on the affluent focuses on providing information helpful to those in financial services. Many of you reading this book will benefit more from information about annual household income and especially how the affluent tend to spend that income. We provide data that is useful for both, but our major emphasis is on the latter.

THE INVESTABLE ASSET VIEW OF AFFLUENCE

NFO Worldgroup defines a *millionaire* household as one having $1 million or more of investable assets, which does not include primary residences, 401(k)s, and other less liquid assets. The number of U.S. millionaire households jumped to 3.8 million in 2003, up from 3.3 million in 2002. That 3.8 million was the highest in the 20 years that NFO has been conducting its surveys. Two facts are important:

1. The number of millionaire households continues to grow.
2. Though at a 20-year high, millionaire households account for only 3.4 percent of the 111 million households in the United States.

The financial services industry is interested in those 3.8 million millionaire households (Who wouldn't be?), but the real affluent opportunity for them lies elsewhere. The Cap Gemini Ernst & Young White Paper of 2002 focuses on what they define as the emerging and mass affluent markets, those with investable assets between $100,000 and $1 million. In terms of financial services, that group has two distinct characteristics:

1. They are forecast to grow at 10 percent to 14 percent a year through 2005, versus a 6 percent growth rate for the $1 million and higher bracket.
2. In terms of financial services, this group remains underserved and untapped.

It is also notable that the average small business owner—one with fewer than 100 employees—has a household income of around $135,000 and assets exceeding $1 million.

THE HOUSEHOLD INCOME VIEW OF AFFLUENCE

The term *household income* is deliberate because it assumes combined income rather than the outdated concept of breadwinner income. With that clarified, there are some important questions to explore if we are to understand the affluent opportunity.

How much does the average American household earn annually? How is wealth distributed among Americans? Who is achieving particular levels of affluence? What is the level of American wealth aspiration these days? What are the chances that the average American can become a millionaire?

Let's begin right in the middle. According to the most recent U.S. census, the median household income is $42,400, and the median per capita income is $22,794. American Demographics has created five income categories to show the income spread in America. We focus on the top three: the super rich, the affluent, and the near affluent. Then we address the "What is the level of American wealth aspiration these days?" question:

- *The super rich—with annual household incomes of $200,000 plus:* Includes about 2.5 million households, or about 2 percent of the population. About one-third are over 55, so their wealth will not likely come from monthly salaries. About 80 percent live in family situations with spouses and children. The super rich include businesspeople and experienced professionals. Many come from the entertainment industry.

- *The affluent—with annual household incomes of $100,000 to $199,000:* Includes about 10.5 million households, or about 10 percent of the population. Most are 45 to 54 and live in large metro areas. However, about 12.1 percent of affluent households are headed by an individual under 35. Though Asian Americans constitute only 3 percent of the population, they represent 5 percent of affluent households. Blacks make up only 5.7 percent, and Whites account for 86 percent. Physicians, financial analysts, and investment bankers are frequently in this category.

- *The near affluent—with annual household incomes of $75,000 to $99,000:* Includes about 10.8 million households or about 10 percent of the population. This group has done well in recent years, growing from 5 percent in 1990. Most are between 35 and 54. In this category are schoolteachers, young professionals, small independent contractors, and employed people with respectable university degrees.

High-income U.S. households are expected to grow at a faster rate than households in general. By 2005, an estimated 17.4 million U.S. households (about 15 percent) will have annual household incomes exceeding $100,000.

Some still assume that our economy is shaped like a pyramid that gets broader toward the bottom as income falls further and further below the $22,794 per capita median income. When thinking *affluent,* they see a small number of prospective customers at the top who are willing to pay top dollar. However, the picture we just painted dispels that notion because the pyramid-shaped economy of bygone days has been replaced by an hourglass economy. Both the low and high ends grow, but the middle is disappearing. This trend is especially evident in the consumer retail market. Wal-Mart and Costco have emerged as the major low-price leaders, while Target has become their upscale rival. Kmart, meanwhile, took the middle road. Unable to compete with Wal-Mart on price or Target on style and quality, Kmart initiated bankruptcy proceedings.

Millions of Americans who once made up the vast middle of the $7 trillion consumer market are migrating upscale toward premium and luxury products and services. This move clearly reflects a shift in consumer aspiration. No one desires to be middle class today; everyone aspires to be at the top. Figure 1.1 summarizes the affluent opportunity.

As we begin looking at the mind of the affluent and creating an affluent selling environment in Chapters 2 and 3, our work would be incomplete if we did not add one more income category to target:

- *The aspiring affluent—many have household incomes of $50,000 or greater per year.* However, this is a group to identify by their expressed and implied aspirations, not their annual income. High-end brands are trying to capitalize on this trend. BMW and Mercedes-Benz are spending billions

Cap Gemni Ernst & Young	Investable Assets	Household Income	
High net worth individuals	$1 to $10 million	Super rich	$200 thousand plus
Mass affluent	$500 thousand to $1 million	Affluent	$100 to $199 thousand
Emerging affluent	$100 to $500 thousand	Near affluent	$75 to $99 thousand
–Untapped and Underserved–		Aspiring affluent	$50 thousand (+ or –)

FIGURE 1.1   The affluent opportunity.

on new, lower priced models to coax customers up from the middle market.

For example, Carl, a 38-year-old engineer, wanted to replace his 1993 Nissan Altima. He set his price at $25,000, but every time he drove another demo car, he pushed his ceiling price up a few thousand. In the end, he purchased a $37,000 BMW 330Ci coupe, which he says won him over with its performance and handling.

Notice what he drove in versus what he drove out. It takes an insightful salesperson to discover this *desire to aspire,* and you will learn how to do that in later chapters.

THE FOCUS OF THIS BOOK

The preceding studies reinforce the need for a how-to book that is designed for immediate practical implementation. Knowing the numbers and some basic characteristics of the super rich down to the aspiring affluent is helpful, but that information simply tells you that a great opportunity exists.

If you or your company is targeting major purchase decision makers, regardless of the products or services involved, your income depends on your ability to get in sync with the major decision-making process of your ideal affluent clientele. Beginning in Chapter 2, we help you do exactly that.

Chapter 2: Getting into the Affluent Mind

It is not that the thinking of affluent people is so different from others. However, because they have the capacity to buy almost anything they want, different factors influence *how* they make buying decisions. This chapter introduces you to the mind of the affluent through the doorway provided by several actual examples. You will discover that the affluent follow a predictable buying pattern and that stress plays an important role in their decision-making process. Pulling it all together, we conclude the chapter by summarizing seven key factors that drive the major purchase decisions of the affluent.

Chapter 3: Creating the Right Sales Environment

Competition for affluent buyers continues to grow, and this chapter helps you understand why. Creating the right sales environment to attract and retain the affluent is becoming increasingly important. Using the affluent buying examples in Chapter 2, we define 10 deficiencies typically found in the sales environment of the affluent encounter. Overcoming these deficiencies is your challenge. As we build on these clues, you are introduced to seven principles for creating a sales environment that will delight your affluent prospects and customers or clients. Conceptual selling is the heart and soul of your success. Four examples from four different industries illustrate creative ways to use concept selling to create the right affluent sales environment for your products and services.

Chapter 4: Overcoming Social Self-Consciousness

Social self-consciousness in salespeople is defined as shunning "prospects of wealth, prestige, power, education, or social standing." According to George Dudley and Shannon Goodson (1999), authors of *The Psychology of Sales Call Reluctance: Earning What You're Worth,* no one is born with social self-consciousness. It is learned, highly contagious, common (documented in 73-plus industries), and can derail an otherwise healthy sales career. If it exists, there is an 87 percent chance that social self-consciousness will plague a salesperson throughout his or her career. But, there is good news: Once detected, it is relatively easy to correct.

If you discover the presence of social self-consciousness through the self-assessment in Chapter 4, you will be able to use the simple action steps provided to assist you in overcoming any aspect of social self-consciousness that might be holding you back.

Chapter 5: Becoming One with the Affluent

You will discover that there is a simple, practical process to becoming one with the affluent. You will learn how to select the right organizations to join and how to get involved in ways that position you to network effectively with affluent members. Chapter 5 includes a detailed outline of the preparation required for involvement in whatever civic organization or group you select. You will also be encouraged to step outside the box and explore the creative strategies two salespeople successfully employed to become one with the affluent.

This process is the first step toward reaching your own goal of becoming one of the affluent.

Chapter 6: Affluent Finishing School

Your critical path to affluent sales success requires mastery of *face-to-face* interaction. Whether it's at a chamber of commerce meeting, a function at your country club, a meeting in your conference room, or a conversation with a prospect on your sales floor, this chapter will help you improve your effectiveness in any face-to-face encounter. You will learn the subtle influence of body language, how to master the first three minutes, ways to introduce yourself, how to project the right image, and five things that should characterize your speaking habits. This chapter is full of practical how-to tactics you can use to succeed.

Chapter 7: Becoming Magnetic

If you are convinced that affluent prospects are searching for what you offer, it's essential that you find a way to attract them to your front door. The issue is dissatisfaction, and you will learn how to use the two main information sources that affluent people depend on to make links between their dissatisfaction and the available solutions. Once you understand those links, you will learn how to master five essential tools to help you capitalize on transforming their dissatisfaction into a sale.

Chapter 8: Becoming Even More Magnetic: Internet Savvy

The Internet has grown from 16 million to over 716 million users in 10 short years, and the fastest growing income group that is on-line are those who earn between $100,000 and $150,000 a year. There are three very important factors that drive Internet use among the affluent, and this chapter details exactly what you can do to turn those factors to your advantage. You will also learn the importance of having your own web site and how to use that web site to create a compelling online presence.

Chapter 9: Mastering Ritz-Carlton Service and FedEx Efficiency

As you seek to deliver a level of service that will delight your customers or clients, it's important to remember that a standard of comparison has already been established in their minds. You may not know exactly what that standard is, but if you benchmark your efforts against Ritz-Carlton service and FedEx efficiency, you can be confident you won't go wrong. Meeting those high standards begins with accepting personal responsibility for the level of service at your location. You will learn six ways to improve those areas that are under your control and how to use a "secret shopper" strategy to find out what your competitors are doing. We also guide you in creating a Value Proposition statement to help you explain to prospects and others what sets you apart.

You cannot establish and successfully implement service and efficiency standards on your own. We show you how to hire and keep the right people, and we provide you with seven ways to make certain you have processes in place that enable the right people to work effectively together.

Chapter 10: The Secret to Affluent Loyalty

Customer satisfaction follow-up phone calls and surveys play an important role in promotional efforts, but they do not measure customer or client loyalty. In this chapter, you will discover why. You will also learn how to effectively measure customer and client loyalty using five specific and observable behaviors. We also provide you with seven principles you can use to initiate strategies that will effectively build loyalty.

Chapter 11: Maximizing Your Affluent
Sales Opportunity

This chapter begins with an important question: What are you going to *do* with what you now know? To answer this question, you first need to determine what you want to accomplish. We call that "envisioning your future," and you will complete an exercise that will help you do precisely that.

How successfully you achieve the future you have envisioned is determined by whether you fall into an *avoidance pattern* or an *achievement pattern*. To make certain it is the latter, you will learn how to activate your achievement cycle by focusing on doing the fixed daily activities that will take you from where you are now to where you want to be 12 months from now. A practical Critical

Path ORGANIZER is provided to help you implement and measure those fixed daily activities on a weekly basis.

Chapter 12: The 12 Commandments of Affluent Selling

These commandments for success in selling to the affluent are a compilation of what you have read here, boiled down into 12 key concepts. These concepts serve as simple reminders of what is most important to your success in selling to the affluent.

THE RESEARCH BEHIND THIS BOOK—2004 AFFLUENT PURCHASING DECISION RESEARCH

We conducted our first affluent research in January 1999. Our purpose was to gain insight into affluent investors' perceptions of the financial professionals who served them. The results were startling. Survey respondents reported significant gaps between what they expected and the performance of their primary financial advisor in 14 of the 20 qualities that they had rated as being most important. On further study, we discovered that this alarming gap was creating a serious erosion in client loyalty. We have been working to help financial professionals close that gap ever since.

Our most recent study, completed as we were beginning this book, had a broader focus. We wanted to answer the question, "What are the key factors that guide the financial management, normal budget, and major item purchase decisions of high-income individuals?" We refer to various aspects of this research (the 2004 Affluent Purchase Decision [APD] Research), throughout the book and have included a brief summary in the Appendix. One of the reasons this research is so relevant for this book is that the respondents' personal annual income levels relate well to the *super rich* and the *affluent* categories described earlier in this chapter: 95.9 percent earn between $100,000 and $500,000 a year, with 82.9 percent in the $100,000 to $249,000 category. Respondents were widely distributed across the six major geographical regions of the United States; 82 percent were between

35 and 64, with 11 percent under age 35; and 82.2 percent were male and 17.8 percent female.

Knowing some relevant statistical facts about the people whom you want to become your customers or clients is helpful, but it is even more important to understand how they think. For that reason, we carefully constructed our 2004 APD Research to help us determine, or at least provide clues to, how the affluent go about making decisions that involve spending money. We wanted to know tendencies, how they think, what leads to the specific actions that occur prior to making a major purchase decision, what the greatest influencers are toward the final decision, and what the affluent appreciate enough, if anything, to help ensure repeat business.

We struck a vein of solid gold. We got answers to all the aforementioned questions and then some. For example, it probably comes as no surprise that insurance coverage is the most important criteria influencing affluent medical decisions. If there is no coverage, the majority will either look elsewhere or forgo the treatment. However, many of you are likely to be as surprised as we were when we discovered that price ranked last in terms of influencing major purchase decisions.

Taken out of context, research can be very misleading, especially when applying regression analysis to identify interrelationships among the variables. So don't think for a New York second that price is not important to affluent consumers. It is extremely important. What we learned about price, though, is its place in the decision making and how closely it is linked to the perceived value of the major purchase. Some of the basic demographic data is more straightforward. When we learn that 22.4 percent of the respondents in our sampling are business owners, you can assume that this has statistical significance to your world. There is a strong probability that a similar percentage of your affluent customers and clients own their own businesses.

So let's start at the beginning, by getting into the mind of the affluent. You are about to find out how they think, which is the subject of the next chapter.

SUMMARY

Two totally different ways of measuring affluence are used: investable assets and household income. The investable asset target market is the emerging and mass affluent markets—those with assets between $100,000 and $1 million. The household income target market includes the super rich with annual incomes of $200,000 plus; the affluent with annual incomes of $100,000 to $199,000; the near affluent with annual household incomes of $75,000 to

---

Research Facts

➤ NFO Worldgroup reports that the number of U.S. millionaire households jumped to 3.8 million in 2003, the highest in 20 years. Millionaire households account for 3.4 percent of the 111 million households in the United States.

➤ Cap Gemini Ernst & Young estimate that the emerging and mass affluent markets (investable assets between $100,000 and $1 million) will grow at a 10 percent to 14 percent rate through 2005.

➤ The super rich includes about 2.5 million households (2 percent of the population).

➤ The affluent category includes about 10.5 million households (10 percent of the population).

➤ The near affluent includes about 10.8 million households (10 percent of the population).

➤ By 2005, an estimated 17.4 million U.S. households (about 15 percent) will have annual household incomes exceeding $100,000.

$99,000; and the aspiring affluent, who will occasionally purchase upscale products and services.

TAKING ACTION

- Explore the demographics in your market area to determine the distribution and, where possible, residential locations of the super rich, affluent, and near affluent market segments.
- Make your personal commitment to journeying down these parallel paths.

2

Getting into the Affluent Mind

The affluent are highly stressed—more than 75 percent of all afflu-ent business owners and self-employed professionals work in excess of 60 hours per week.

—FACTOID, 2004 APD RESEARCH

The art of selling to the affluent requires a blend of expertise, imagination, method, inventiveness, and finesse. Equally important, it requires focus. The growing affluent opportunity does not exist simply because of the numbers. Most of the affluent people you will target are not those who have inherited wealth and remain holed up in their enclaves, willing to associate only with "their own." Rather, they are generators and earners of wealth, many of whom have emerged from middle-American backgrounds to acquire first-generation wealth. Our 2004 APD Research focused on exactly that group of self-made affluence: 22.4 percent are business owners, 25.9 percent are self-employed professionals, and 44.9 percent are high-paid executives and commissioned employees (salespeople). As you can see from the factoid at the beginning of the chapter, they are also hard workers.

The affluent are similar in many ways to other Americans from the neighborhoods and backgrounds of their childhood. At the same time, their experiences of gaining and living in a world of affluence have changed them. They are more focused, more committed to their careers, more clear about their goals, and willing to pay the price to achieve.

Selling successfully to the affluent begins with getting into the affluent mind. See if you can figure out the best way to approach the couple described next.

Bob started his business over 20 years ago, has done well for himself, is a hard worker, and likes to purchase the finer things in life. Every couple of years, both he and his wife Mary turn in their leased luxury automobiles for new models. For the past 10 years, because of both convenience and quality, they drove the same make automobile from the same dealership.

This year, Bob and Mary both made a change. Bob attributed it to not liking the new styling. His wife was more revealing about the decision. "If the sales guy would have made Bob feel like a big shot, he would have had two customers. The poor guy must have been new." Bob leased a different make of luxury car at another dealership that was a 30-minute drive into the suburbs. Mary chose a convertible sports car at a local dealer.

A short time later, Mary had a flat tire. Since her car was a high-performance sports car, the warranty stipulated that only the dealership could fix the flat. Though it seemed odd, Mary accepted the stipulation. This is where the adventure began. A week later, Mary found herself stranded with a second flat on the same tire. Bob was out of town on business when he received a panicked call from Mary. She was now afraid to drive the car. Bob called the dealership's service department to find out what was going on. The service manager explained that the tire must be defective. Probing further, Bob discovered they did not replace her original tire but merely patched it. When he asked why, the manager told him it was a high-performance tire that the dealership didn't keep in stock. The manager offered to put Mary into a loaner car for whatever time it took to get a tire but would not guarantee a date. After a heated exchange, one that Bob has repeated blow-by-blow to anyone who will listen, he told the dealership to keep the car. He then proceeded to buy out the lease at a cost of $8,000, and Mary went back to their original dealer for a different model. Bob loves his new luxury car, but the suburban dealership is too inconvenient for his taste. He will go elsewhere when his lease is up, if not sooner.

Welcome to the affluent person's world of major purchase decision making. Like most self-made small business owners, Bob is always looking for a deal. Sure, he buys luxury items, and he prides himself on never paying full price. Yet, he just lost a substantial amount of money on a dispute over a tire, more than he saved on the price of both vehicles combined.

There are ample lessons in Bob's story to write an entire training program on what *not to do* when selling and servicing the affluent. Bob could have saved himself a lot of grief, not to mention money, if he had kept his healthy ego in line when dealing with the first salesperson. But he didn't, and he can afford not to if he so chooses. Like most hard chargers, Bob likes being fussed over when making a major purchase. It's an important dimension of his decision process. He also insists on a high level of professionalism. The fact that this "poor salesperson" (Mary's description) was new to the luxury car business didn't cut it. The dealership had the salesperson on the showroom floor without proper training, assuming that selling cars was simply that—selling cars. When it comes to selling to the affluent, there is nothing "simple" about it.

The service department handling Mary's sports car could become a Comedy Central skit. They couldn't have done more things wrong if they had just finished reading a book titled *How to Intentionally Run Off Affluent Customers.* The tire was not fixed properly the first time. Rather than plead *mea culpa* and provide limo service and whatever Mary wanted, the service manager made the serious mistake of arguing with Bob. Equally important, the salesperson who originally sold Mary the luxury sports car was never brought into the picture.

Bob, who considers himself an extremely price-value consumer, took an $8,000 hit on his wife's convertible sports car. According to our 2004 APD Research, Bob's behavior is no surprise. Finding a discounted sales price ranked much lower than finding the right set of features and finding the best possible option after careful evaluation and comparison among our survey participants. When affluent respondents were given the opportunity to write in other criteria they considered important when making major purchase decisions, the quality of the warranty or guarantee had the most influence by a wide margin.

The art of selling to the affluent goes far beyond simply making a sale, although you do have to make the sale. It involves discovering how the individual makes major purchase buying decisions and then being able to uncover any hidden issues. It also requires making certain that postsale service is more than what is advertised. Our research made this very clear. The two most important factors influencing whether the affluent would use the same product or service provider again when making a major purchase were:

1. Any problems I encountered were resolved quickly and satisfactorily.
2. They provided good service following my purchase.

When selling to the affluent, you don't simply manage the sale; you manage the relationship. Here's another example.

In the midst of writing this chapter, my wife scheduled a dental appointment for me. Since I had not been to the dentist in a few years, she insisted that I go. Fitting into a profile similar to Bob, I wanted to get this appointment over quickly. After all, I have a consulting practice to run. My trip to the dentist was anything but quick. Here's what happened.

My appointment began to veer off course even before it began. The receptionist called my office and requested that I come 15 minutes early to fill out some paperwork that was required due to my four-year absence. That struck me as odd. After all, this dental office had been attending to my family's dental needs for over 25 years. With three children and a wife who have required some serious dental work, they had done very well by us.

I arrived early, completed the form, and was escorted into the same room where I've had my teeth cleaned many times. The dental hygienist was new and very pleasant, so I was very patient in the beginning when she asked for permission to complete a "new patient" dental profile form. The truth be told, I do not like forms, and I had already arrived early and filled one out. I began to think, "What is going on here?"

As I settled into the dental chair, the young hygienist sat on a stool, clipboard in hand, and proceeded to ask me with a straight face, "On a 1 to 10 scale, with 10 being excellent, how would you rate your smile?" Incredulous, and feigning not hearing the question, I asked her to repeat it. She did, and I answered, "9 or 10." After dutifully recording my response, she asked, "Why did you say 9?" Suddenly, I realized what was going on and felt foolish for not picking up on it earlier. I was being pitched. She was going to use this profile to sell me on some type of cosmetic dentistry program. I responded by asking what they charge for teeth whitening.

That concluded my profile, but the teeth cleaning I had expected was still not to be. I was told I needed a full set of x-rays. This made sense because it had been a while since I had been there. Ten x-rays later and counting, I stopped the hygienist and asked how many x-rays she was planning to take. When she answered that a full set was 18 x-rays, I bolted upright and asked for time out. I don't like unnecessary radiation going through my body, and I have never had more than four x-rays taken of my teeth at one time in my entire life. I calmly explained that I simply wanted my teeth cleaned, and that was the beginning of the end. The hygienist informed me that would require another visit because this one was for a "new patient" examination, which was not what I had expected when taking time out of my busy schedule to go there.

I will not bore you with any more details other than to say the dentist, a new face as she had recently purchased the dental practice from my original dentist, caught up with me as I was leaving. She apologized and explained that this is the "new" school of dentistry. She then escorted me back to my dental chair and in-structed the hygienist to clean my teeth.

Much like Bob's luxury automobile experience, I have retold my dental saga to anyone who would listen. It annoys me even to write about it. Currently, I am in the process of changing dentists. I have nothing against cosmetic dentistry. I have two beautiful daughters who have already gone through the whitening drill on my dime. What bothered me was the deception and the insensitivity.

Bob's and my stories, though somewhat dramatic, are not as unique as you might think. Here is another bizarre tale. Imagine investing $5 million through a financial advisor and then three years later, having your nest egg down to $2.5 million. That's what happened to Carol, and as you might expect, she was looking for a new financial advisor. Through someone in her church, she was referred to Jack, a fellow parishioner.

On the surface, this might appear to be a fairly simple case. Client has money; client loses 50 percent following the advice of someone she paid to provide such advice; dissatisfaction reaches a boiling point; client actively searches for an alternative. This should be an easy sell for Jack, but the fact is, he nearly blew it.

Jack saw immediately that the investments recommended by Carol's former advisor were selected for their healthy fees, not their suitability. He immediately assumed this was the problem, so he launched into his typical risk tolerance and asset allocation pitch. "It finally dawned on me that I was losing her when her eyes started glazing over," was the way Jack explained it to me. Out of desperation, he asked the obvious question: "Tell me again, why are you dissatisfied with your financial advisor?" Expecting to hear a tale of woe about her lost millions, he was shocked when Carol instead talked about being passed off to the advisor's son while the advisor vacationed in Barbados. As Jack recounted the story, he said, "You know, not once did she complain about her losses."

Another anomaly? Perhaps, but the art of selling to the affluent is full of anomalies. Many who write about the affluent tend to focus on their investment habits. The fact is, some invest well, others invest poorly, and still others spend much of what they bring in. Some live below their means, while others, like Bob, live quite well. What they share in common is that they all earn more, have more liquid cash and, to get what they want, will pay you more commissions or fees than 82 percent of their fellow citizens. For those who understand how they think, the affluent are the sweet spot.

The affluent follow a predictable buying pattern. They do their research, most often online, and then they go wherever the products and services they want are conveniently available at the best price—including discount warehouse clubs, as amazing as that may seem. In fact, 75.8 percent of our survey respondents said that finding the best option through careful evaluation and comparison was very important to them when making major purchase decisions. Here are two examples:

1. Tom and Joyce recently went to their local Costco warehouse club, but not to buy in bulk to get the lowest price, as many Sam's Club and Costco shoppers do. "We find things there that we don't find in regular grocery stores," says Joyce, 59, a pension plan administrator, "like frozen crème brulee and onion soup bread bowls."
2. Karen, a 28-year-old public relations rep, loves to show off her half-carat diamond earrings given to her by her husband, who purchased them for $170 at BJ's Wholesale Club. "It's the thought that counts," is Karen's reasoning.

The irony is that the more successful and affluent people are, the more stressful their lives become. The American Express/Roper ASW survey (2003) reported that 66 percent of affluent Americans experience high levels of stress, the highest among the 11 countries surveyed.

High levels of stress take a psychological and physical toll on everyone. The major differences lie in how people deal with it:

- Some hard chargers take pride in the persona of being able to handle high levels of stress. These people talk about all of their responsibilities, the number of people who depend on them, and the projects that only they can oversee. Do not mistake this as a cry for sympathy. These people are trying to impress you, so be impressed.
- Other affluent individuals are in a state of stress denial. Rather than brag about the stress in their lives, they simply accept it as normal. I do not mean to infer that their stress, or the way they suppress it, is healthy—but it quietly exists.
- Many are able to recognize their excessive levels of stress and understand that left unchecked it can be harmful. They attempt to deal with it through counseling, self-help books, yoga, exercise, and the like.

Whatever form of stress-carrying affluent consumers you might encounter, it is important to be aware that stress impacts who they are, their emotional state of mind, and how they go about major purchase decisions. You are dealing not only with savvy, skeptical, price-conscious consumers; they are typically stressed out to boot! This is an important gem of information to keep tucked away in your mind. How do you deal with someone who is under tremendous stress? With kid gloves, that's how!

For a moment, forget about selling and recall the last time you witnessed someone (not you, I hope) involved in road rage. To be sure, it's an ugly scene. Nine out of ten times, the person who lost it, the temporarily insane driver, feels tremendous remorse and embarrassment when he or she finally recovers. What you witnessed was a high-level stress attack in what would typically be considered a normal person. Driving, regardless of our affluence, has become a high-stress affair. The same can be said of major purchase decisions. Too many options with too much information to digest in too little time, and the high levels of stress that might be momentarily dormant suddenly become stirred up.

When people are under a lot of stress, they look for relief. They initiate many major purchase decisions to reward themselves for their hard work—a stress release. The last thing they want is a hassle. Don't be fooled by that composed and somewhat intimidating affluent customer standing in front of you or talking on the other end of the phone. As they say where I grew up in White Plains, New York, "Life is a head-fake."

As much as these hard chargers are cynical and savvy, much of their major purchase decision making is emotional. If they like you, if it feels right, if you make them feel important and in control, and if you help them think that they have made a well-informed decision, they are likely to conduct business with you. But this will not let you off the hook. You had better know your product and your field well, because once the affluent make this emotional decision, they will go to great lengths to support it with logic.

Can you imagine Bob telling a golfing buddy, "Yeah, I leased my new car at a dealership 30 minutes out of town because I liked the salesman." It will never happen. Bob will tell his buddy every benefit and every feature he can remember to posture himself as a savvy consumer. Then the emotional dimension reenters the picture. Bob will then attempt to sell his buddy on purchasing a similar vehicle at the same dealership from the same salesperson. Why? It's called emotional income. If Bob can get a friend or two or three to contact that salesperson, he receives logical confirmation of his major purchase decision. Buyer's remorse becomes nonexistent.

WHAT DRIVES MAJOR PURCHASE DECISION MAKING

The Census Bureau claims that the baby-boom bubble has reached the point where more American households have some level of affluence than ever before. Translated, that means more money is being invested, and more major purchase decisions are being made. Salespeople interested in making a living in the world of the affluent—and it can be an excellent living—must be in tune with all the subtle nuances that drive those purchase decisions.

These are dedicated, hard-working, busy people. They are focused on their work, whether it's running their business, climbing the corporate ladder, or staying current in their profession. Note the hours worked as reported by our 2004 APD Research respondents (see Table 2.1).

The affluent never have enough time in the day to finish all of their work. When making a purchase decision, they expect minimal hassles and big-time attention. At least seven factors typically drive the major purchase decision-making process of the affluent:

1. They want to be respected, and even honored, for the level of success they have achieved.
2. They are successful because of the professionalism and competence they apply to their work, and they expect no less from others.
3. They will react strongly to any efforts to deceive or manipulate them, and when that happens, they will likely take their business elsewhere.
4. They will do the research and trust their own judgment to define value in their own terms. Then they will go wherever that quest for value takes them, even if it is a web site or a warehouse club.

TABLE 2.1   Number of hours worked per week by the affluent.

Hours	Percent
Over 60	25.9
50 to 60	32.3
40 to 50	24.4
40 or less	17.4

5. Instead of striving to keep up with the Joneses, the affluent today want to be different from the Joneses.
6. They experience enough tension and hassles in their daily work life, and they want to be free from all of that when dealing with people who would like to sell them something.
7. They can afford and are willing to pay for the best information, the best products, the highest level of competence, and the best professional service available.

Failure to understand these seven drivers of major purchase decision making by the affluent will significantly hamper your sales career. What makes dealing with the affluent more of an art than a science is the complexity of their decision making. They do not like salespeople, yet they need to be sold. They are well-informed consumers, often spending hours doing Internet research before making a major purchase. Although emotion plays a major part in their decision making, they often couch it all in logical verbiage.

Mastering the art of selling to the affluent requires that you learn how to create a sales environment that captures the heart and mind of the affluent. In the next chapter, we help you address this important issue.

SUMMARY

Most of the affluent you target will be business owners, self-employed professionals, and high-paid executives and commissioned employees (successful salespeople). Selling successfully to the affluent begins with getting into the affluent mind. The art of selling to the affluent goes far beyond simply making a sale, but you do have to make the sale—once you have discovered how the individual makes buying decisions.

When selling to the affluent, you don't simply manage the sale; you manage the relationship. The affluent follow a predictable buying pattern. They do their research, most often online, and then go wherever the products and services they want are conveniently available at the best price.

The irony is that the more successful and affluent people are, the more stressful their life becomes. Some handle stress well, others are in a state of stress denial, and many recognize their excessive levels of stress and deal with it. When under stress, people look for relief. People initiate many major purchase decisions to reward themselves for hard work—as a stress release.

Research Facts

➢ Of the respondents, 93.2 percent were self-made: 22.4 percent were business owners, 25.9 percent were self-employed professionals, and 44.9 percent were high-paid executive and commissioned employees (successful salespeople).

➢ Finding the best option through careful evaluation was very important to 75.8 percent of survey respondents when making major purchase decisions.

➢ In a survey of 300 high school children in private schools, more than 90 percent said that they see their parents as living under enormous stress, and they expect to do the same. "At Home, School, Give Kids a Stress Break" by Dan Gottlieb, *Philadelphia Inquirer*, September 20, 2004.

➢ The hours worked by our respondents were: 25.9 percent, over 60 hours; 32.3 percent, 50 to 60 hours; 24.4 percent, 40 to 50 hours; 17.4 percent, 40 hours or less.

➢ When making a major purchase, 39.8 percent of affluent consumers consider finding a discounted or sales price as "very important."

➢ When making a major purchase, 83.3 percent of affluent consumers insist on finding the right set of features.

Seven factors typically drive the major purchase decision-making process of the affluent: They desire to be respected for the success they have achieved; they expect the same level of professionalism and competence they apply to their work; they react strongly to being deceived or manipulated; they trust their own research and judgment, and they define value in their own terms; they want to be different from the Joneses; they want to be free from tension and hassles when dealing with salespeople; and they can afford and will pay for only the best.

TAKING ACTION

- Begin immediately to become proactive in your efforts to find and contact affluent prospects.
- Observe how your current affluent customers or clients make their buying decisions, noting how much research they have done before approaching you.
- Make certain you are an expert in your products, your services, and your company.
- Make certain that every feature and benefit of your product and service is exactly as advertised.
- Begin listing what differentiates your products and services from your competition, especially in terms of the benefits your affluent customers or clients will receive.

3

CREATING THE RIGHT SALES ENVIRONMENT

Offering the lowest price has the least influence on whether the affluent will conduct future business with you.

—Factoid, 2004 APD Research

With the mid-range of the consumer market diminishing in this hourglass economy, retail stores, specialty shops, dealerships, and service providers everywhere are focusing upscale in an effort to attract affluent buyers. But as the examples in Chapter 2 illustrate, it takes more than a high-priced product or service to capture the hearts and minds of the affluent. As the competition for affluent buyers grows, creating the right sales environment will become increasingly important.

Bob and Mary are affluent buyers who are still looking for a luxury car dealership with the right sales environment. The deficiencies they encountered provide a rich set of clues for what that will take:

- After driving the same make automobile from the same dealership for 10 years, Bob was ready to switch.

   Clue 1: "If the sales guy had made Bob feel like a big shot . . ." It's called *neglect.* Loyal affluent customers are the product of established and proactively built relationships. Whether the luxury automobile dealership management neglected this critical issue in their sales training or simply spent too much time teaching their salespeople the features and benefits of their products rather than making certain they understood the important features of their affluent clientele, they lost Bob. He was not made to feel special, there was no attempt at relationship building, and he found the features and benefits he wanted in a luxury automobile elsewhere.

• Mary's flat tire stranded her. The dealer did not replace her original defective tire; he merely patched it.

Clue 2: The reason given was that they don't stock this high-performance tire. In other words, dealer convenience was more important than customer convenience. The dealer has not learned that service quality is a critical factor in proactively building long-term relationships with affluent customers. Our 2004 APD Research clearly revealed that the most important criterion for strengthening loyalty and ensuring repeat business is resolving problems quickly and satisfactorily.

It's difficult to imagine a place of business that caters to the affluent blowing such a golden opportunity. This dealership not only lost out on Mary's potential of becoming a loyal repeat customer but also lost the power of her positive word-of-mouth influence, as well as Bob's. It does not take a microscopic inspection to recognize the opportunity lost by not resolving problems from the perspective of their affluent clientele.

• Mary's defective high-performance tire would take an unknown length of time to replace.

Clue 3: The manager offered to provide a loaner car for whatever time it took to replace the tire, but he would not guarantee a date. That failure to commit and act reeks of complacency and inefficiency. The dealer has not learned that Ritz-Carlton-level service with FedEx efficiency is the only standard the affluent will accept.

Building on Clue 2 and being able to resolve problems quickly and satisfactorily, our research exposed another statistically significant factor for generating loyalty and repeat business—providing good service following the purchase. How difficult would it have been for Mary's original salesperson to take responsibility for getting her a new tire? Whether he had to drive to another dealership or purchase the tire with his own money, this level of service would have had significant impact on Mary's becoming a repeat customer.

- Bob loves his new luxury car, but the dealer's suburban location is too inconvenient for his taste.

  Clue 4: That dealer (among others) is like the fisherman who announces to the fish, "If you want to get caught, come on over to my pond next Saturday at 10 A.M." Location is one of the top five "very important" criteria impacting the purchase decisions of the affluent. Some luxury dealerships have figured this out and offer a form of valet service. But most simply provide a loaner car. They have not learned that the best way to catch affluent customers is to go where they are at a time that is convenient for them.

Do you know any car dealers, luxury or otherwise, who have a fully equipped van they will send to your office to service your car while you are at work? Bob's new luxury dealership provides him with a luxury loaner vehicle while his car is being serviced, but it is still, in his estimation, 90 minutes out of his busy schedule. At first glance you might feel sorry for the salespeople in these situations. Don't. Bob's salesperson earned a healthy commission and could easily have provided the necessary valet service. By picking up his car and delivering the loaner, the salesperson could have made Bob a customer for life. After all, Bob loves the car.

Medical practices are notorious for repetitious paperwork and keeping you waiting long past your appointment time. That's why I grit my teeth (unintended pun) whenever I have to go to the dentist or any medical office, for that matter. But even I did not anticipate what I experienced during my recounted visit to the dentist.

- Not at the time the appointment was made, but days later, the dental office called to ask me to come in 15 minutes early to complete paperwork because of my four-year absence.

    Clue 5: My entire family uses this dental clinic—frequently. In this age of computers and networking, they could have checked a few items on the phone to update their system with the few personal data items they needed. When targeting affluent families, your system needs to be state-of-the-art for exactly that purpose.

The old adage, "Know your customer or client," is at the heart of this clue. They not only failed to check my records but also ended up wasting my time. These were two critical mistakes that could easily have been avoided with a more patient-centric approach.

- "On a scale of 1 to 10, with 10 being excellent, how would you rate your smile?"

    Clue 6: Only someone who is intimidated by being in a medical office or who is incredibly patient and nice would tolerate this type of manipulation and deception for very long. I went to have my teeth cleaned. That's what I wanted. But they were concerned only with their agenda—manipulating me into signing up for a cosmetic dental program.

Such tactics are based on the fact that people who can't afford it sometimes can be coerced into buying it anyway. Heck, today's dental clinics offer payment plans. However, the affluent, who can afford these services, will be receptive only when the benefits are presented in an open and honest way, complete with a clear explanation of the costs involved.

- This is the "new school" of dentistry.

    Clue 7: The new dentist apologized and then asked the hygienist to do what I asked for in the first place—clean my teeth. Great, except for one thing. She tried to justify the hygienist's actions by giving it a nice-sounding contemporary label.

The affluent are impressed with honest performance, not deceptive labels. Since my "new school of dentistry" experience, I have discovered that I am not alone in my annoyance. Albeit purely anecdotal, it seems that the affluent are not pleased with this new school of dentistry and its bill-padding procedures.

Carol's unhappiness with her financial advisor provides a few more important clues to successfully working with the affluent.

- Jack saw that the investments recommended by Carol's former advisor were selected for their healthy fees, not their suitability.

  Clue 8: Jack assumed there was a single, obvious reason for Carol's dissatisfaction, so he immediately tried to convince her that he had the solution. Jack failed to recognize that with affluence comes a multitude of interwoven financial, family, and personal needs that require the advice and guidance of a skilled financial professional.

The source of Carol's dissatisfaction is buried somewhere in that multitude of needs. With affluent prospects, you must ask until you think you fully understand and then continue to ask as they respond. Our 2004 APD Research provides a clear picture of what is important to Carol. She wants whoever is advising her on her finances to understand her goals and her family situation before offering any form of investment advice. It sounds like common sense, but neither Jack nor Carol's previous advisor paid attention to this extremely important set of criteria.

- Jack launched into his typical risk tolerance and asset allocation pitch until he noticed Carol's eyes starting to glaze over.

  Clue 9: Jack did the worst thing you can do with an affluent prospect; he slipped immediately into his salesperson role. Affluent people are typically confident of their decision-making ability. They do not want to be sold; they want to be served and assisted as they move through the decision-making process. Another issue that may have almost derailed Jack's efforts was using technical jargon that Carol did not fully understand. Everyone wants things explained in language that is familiar to them. The affluent have too much buying power to tolerate anything less. What our 2004 ADP Research also told us, and Jack obviously didn't have a clue about, is that when it came to the big picture of her financial affairs, Carol was like the respondents in our survey where specific investment decisions ranked below having a formal financial plan and making certain that all her financial documents were organized and coordinated. Properly applied, knowledge can be powerful. In the world of the affluent, it can accelerate your journey to personal affluence.

• When Jack finally did ask Carol why she was dissatisfied with her advisor, Carol said nothing about her lost millions. Instead, she talked about being passed off to the advisor's son while the advisor vacationed in Barbados.

Clue 10: Jack did not recognize that regardless of how unhappy Carol might be with her investment losses, her greatest concern was the nature and quality of the professional relationship she had with her advisor. The flippant way he passed her off was simply the last straw. Affluent investors understand the impact that the events of September 11, 2001, corporate corruption, and the declining market have had on their investments. What they want is a competent financial advisor who will walk down that path with them, providing immediate personal attention to whatever needs arise. When asked about selecting their primary financial coordinator, 69.8 percent of our survey respondents said that being proactive about contacting them when upcoming tax and other changes will impact their investment portfolio was very important to them. And yet, this is where the largest gap existed between their expectations and the performance of their present financial coordinator.

If you want 10 ways to drive affluent prospects and customers away, take a lesson from the preceding clues and create a sales environment that emphasizes:

1. Neglect
2. Poor service quality
3. Complacency and inefficiency
4. Inconveniences
5. Technical deficiencies
6. Manipulation
7. Deceit
8. Telling, not listening
9. Technical jargon
10. Impersonal relationship

It would be logical to assume that a car showroom, dental office, and financial advisor's office present very different environments for "selling" products and services. But as you go back through the 10 clues and think about how each clue can be applied to each of these settings, you see that they have more in common than meets the eye. As we combine these clues with the five factors that typically drive major purchases from Chapter 2, a picture of the sales environment that will attract and retain the affluent begins to emerge. We call that picture the *affluent sales environment.*

THE AFFLUENT SALES ENVIRONMENT

The affluent sales environment is driven by the following seven principles:

1. *Proactive relationship-building principle:* From the initial contact forward, your emphasis must be to take the initiative and proactively build a long-term, professional relationship:

- Everyone in your office or organization who sells and supports must understand and be fully engaged in the process of building long-term professional relationships.
- Salespeople must be the point persons in this relationship-building process, so turnover must be reduced to the absolute minimum.

While writing this chapter, I took a break and went to a local upscale supermarket with my son Patrick. I was picking up some last-minute items for a cookout that evening. As we approached the checkout lane, the cashier and the bagger (that person who asks "Plastic or paper?") were engaged in an ongoing conversation. Thinking to myself that this behavior was rather rude, I simply paid for the items and we left. A couple of days later when I was being complimented about my daughter Amy's customer focus (she had a summer job at a local sporting goods store), Patrick, who also heard the compliment, commented about the rudeness of the cashier and bagger from two days before. And Patrick is only 14. Little things mean a lot, and most of what it takes to meet and exceed the expectations of your affluent clientele is not complicated.

2. *Convenience principle:* You must initiate contact and be able to deliver everything you offer at a time and place that is convenient to the customer:

- You must be prepared to go to your customers rather than waiting for them to come to you—to sell, deliver, and service.
- Your store, showroom, or office hours must be replaced with a 24/7/365 mind-set, if not availability.

As basic as this principle might appear, it's important to always keep in mind the number of hours that the majority of affluent consumers work in any given week and the level of stress to which they regularly subject themselves. Will they travel to get what they want? Yes, if they are forced to. Is convenience a consideration that impacts affluent purchasing decisions? Absolutely, and with statistically proven significance. Your role as a professional salesperson catering to the affluent is to do everything within your control to make certain that convenience is a perceived reality in the mind of your clientele.

3. *Seamless selling principle:* Your selling process and skills must unfold naturally, and your effort to close the sale must be the logical conclusion of everything that went before:

- You must replace your "sales pitch" with a questioning process that provides you with vital information about your customers and their families while helping them discover how what you offer can successfully satisfy their needs and desires.
- Any intent or suggestion of manipulation and deception must be eliminated from your selling process.

In other words, even though you are selling, if you give yourself away and come across as a salesperson, you have lost. The affluent are very strong in their likes and dislikes. Topping their list of dislikes are paying taxes and dealing with salespeople. At the same time, these savvy consumers recognize the importance of the sales role. They just prefer that salespeople apply their craft with the highest level of professionalism possible.

The best disguise for your sales effort is to frame everything as consultative. Your role is to consult with prospects and assist them in making their major purchase decision. A convergence of skills is at work in order to be seamless. You must be able to develop rapport and get to know your prospect by skillfully asking questions. Many sales organizations refer to this as *profiling*. You then complement this fact finding with product knowledge, the inner workings of your firm, the competitive alternatives, price-point alternatives, warranty guidelines and comparisons, and so on. Your challenge is to naturally fit your product or service to the customer's needs and wants. This conceptual selling is the essence of the seamless selling process.

4. *The quality principle:* Every product and service you sell must be upscale, both in terms of the options offered and the quality of those options:

- What you offer must enable affluent customers and clients to create something that is uniquely theirs.
- You must make everything clear and easily understood, remembering that affluent prospects normally have already done their homework.
- Everything must work exactly the way it is intended.

Our 2004 APD Research raised a warning flag for the financial services industry. Although affluent consumers are interested in their financial affairs, they are not turning to banks or financial advisors (stockbrokers) or insurance agents for advice and counsel. We used 10 criteria relating to selecting a primary banking service and eight criteria for selecting a primary financial coordinator (advisor, consultant, professional). Even though these institutions, especially banks and large financial institutions such as the major wirehouses, have spent hundreds of millions of dollars in advertising, upgrading technology to better service the affluent, and training their financial advisors and consultants how to better work with affluent clients, the affluent are not buying it. Somehow there appears to be a disconnect between what is perceived as the final product in the mind of the affluent and what these financial entities are promoting.

At this particular juncture between affluent financial needs and wants and the opportunity therein, the financial world could learn a valuable and priceless lesson by studying the U.S. luxury automobile market. There once was a time, long ago, when the General

Motors luxury line was synonymous with "best in class." Whenever something was referred to as the "Cadillac of . . ."—whether it was toasters, lawn mowers, or fountain pens—the reference was clear. It was the best. Yet over the past few decades, Cadillac has lost its hold on the luxury car market to a number of Japanese companies. There are too many factors to detail here, but one is important relative to the quality principle being discussed. General Motors "branded" Cadillac as an inferior product when, because of the competition and slipping sales, they invested heavily in promoting the Cadillac line while failing to invest enough in the vehicle to make certain that it regained its stature as the best in class.

The affluent were not fooled, nor were they amused, when they discovered that the car they had purchased was not the quality they expected. The result was a loss in market share that is unlikely to be regained because the public no longer trusts that General Motors can develop a true luxury car. Recently, while glancing through one of the automotive magazines in an airport newsstand, I noticed it had rated five luxury automobiles. I was surprised to find a particular model of Cadillac rated first in terms of performance and price/value. I would love to see General Motors reclaim the high ground once again, but they have an uphill challenge.

5. *Ritz-Carlton service principle.* You must be as concerned with providing quality service *after* the sale as you are with the quality of what you sell. As Horst Schulze, president and COO of Ritz-Carlton Hotels for 18 years, explains, "One of the great paradoxes of our aging service economy is that actual service has disappeared from most American companies. The service most of us encounter these days is virtual, supplied by voice mail, e-mail, satellite pagers, and, of course, the Internet. Consumers are noticing the difference. Never mind that these enterprises are offering innovative products and services. Their common failing is they haven't learned to treat their customers the way they themselves would like to be treated."— *Since When Did I Ask to Help Myself?* by Horst Schulze, *New York Times,* 2002.

- Everything must be done right the first time.
- You must never assume that affluent customers are satisfied.
- You must see this principle as an extension of principle 1—to proactively build a long-term professional relationship.

On a personal level, my hotel of choice when I travel is the Ritz-Carlton. What I like is the consistency of the experience. Every staff member is well trained, very helpful, extremely efficient, and has the authority to resolve problems on the spot. I can remember one particular incident when I asked for a 6:00 A.M. wake-up call. My intention was to go to the fitness center and exercise before getting caught up in my day. The wake-up call was on time, and I was asked which newspaper I preferred plus whether I would like a pot of coffee delivered with my paper of choice. Impressed, I selected two papers and accepted their offer for a pot of coffee. I returned from my workout around 7:00 A.M. and found my papers, a luke-warm pot of coffee, and a bill for $15.00 for the coffee.

I know that $15.00 for a pot of coffee that you get free at a Courtyard Marriott doesn't seem to fit the mold of Ritz-Carlton service. But it was the resolution of the problem that sets the Ritz-Carlton apart. I stopped by the front desk and mentioned the misunderstanding over the coffee charge. The person I talked with had the authority to immediately remove it from my bill. He also informed me about the hours of their complimentary coffee stand that was set up in the lobby. My problem was resolved quickly and to my satisfaction, the ongoing service was outstanding, and I am still singing the praises of Ritz-Carlton service and frequenting their properties whenever possible.

As you know, problem resolution and ongoing high-level service have the greatest impact on repeat business and positive word-of-mouth influence. It's called *customer loyalty.*

6. *FedEx efficiency principle:* All interactions must occur in a hassle-free, upbeat, respectable, and highly efficient manner. Your affluent customers and clients will expect nothing less:

- Your information systems must be state-of-the-art, and you must have the technical support to keep them operating 24/7/365.
- You must eliminate all unnecessary paperwork and do everything possible to eliminate the need for a prospect or customer to spend time filling out forms. Figuring out how to do this will be a challenge, but it will be worth it.
- You must constantly measure everything you do according to the two critical efficiency measures: the time it takes and the number of errors that occurred.

As a salesperson, it is easy to fall into the trap of bemoaning all the inner workings of your company that are beyond your immediate control. Beware of this trap because it will keep you from providing service with FedEx efficiency. The real issue involves understanding the strengths and weaknesses of your company, managing the expectations of your customers and clients, and making certain that you do everything within your control to make things go smoothly.

If you consider yourself to be a salesperson as well as a high-priced problem solver, you are one step ahead of the game. In terms of problem solving, an ounce of prevention is worth a pound of cure. My advice is to make certain that every customer, client, and prospect knows that you are their "go-to" trouble shooter, and it is your responsibility to make certain everything proceeds according to plan. Toward that end, you will find it very profitable to give your cell phone number or pager number with 24/7 access to every affluent customer or client.

7. *Integrity principle:* Your affluent sales environment must have the appearance, feel, and experience of being an integrated whole:

- From the initial contact on, the prospect/customer/client must never be passed on from one individual to another.

- Everything must be customized to each individual's particular needs.
- You must continually look for new ways to service each individual.

Many factors go into how a person makes an integrity assessment. One of the more subtle, but nevertheless very real, factors is consistent congruence. It takes only one disconnect, whether it is a messy bathroom, a bad cup of coffee, or an employee with a bad attitude. Anything that might be perceived as inconsistent with the first-class quality you are trying to project will plant a seed of distrust. Once planted, this seed is difficult to weed out.

Although these are the seven key pieces of the affluent sales environment puzzle, there's more to the puzzle. In addition to having all the pieces in place, a finished puzzle provides an aesthetic quality that creates a memorable picture. In fact, keeping the box cover with that picture in front of you is what encourages you to keep working to create what you see. Whatever pieces you put together in the affluent sales environment you create must also blend together to provide a memorable experience.

If you enter a Wal-Mart or Costco, you step into a sales environment where products are sold as commodities, with an emphasis on function and price. You will find a few high-priced items, but mostly you will see branded products that serve functional needs and appeal to moderate-income homeowners. Commodity selling produces a level of price competition that shrinks profit margins and makes it difficult for commissioned salespeople to acquire affluence. Because of this, the sales environment that these companies and salespeople operate in, although it is very functional for their purposes, is not designed to cater to the affluent.

According to our 2004 APD Research, when affluent clients are involved with a major purchase decision, finding the lowest price is not the dominant criterion that impacts the final choice. And as much as people talk about price, it ranks significantly lower than offering the right set of features and finding the best possible option through careful evaluation and comparison. Only 39.8 percent rated finding a discounted or sale price as very important, compared to 83.3 percent for the right features and 75.8 percent for careful evaluation and comparison (see Table 3.1).

The growing affluent opportunity is making it possible for many to rise above the rat race of price competition, but it requires the creation of a dramatically different sales environment. Instead of selling television sets, you must switch to selling entertainment. Get the picture?

If you do get the picture, you have mentally transitioned from selling a commodity to selling a concept. Instead of stressing function and price, you help your prospective customer achieve his or her dreams by promoting ideas, beauty, pride, and a level of personal attention that leads to a long-term relationship.

Concept selling is the heart and soul of an affluent sales environment. It is being used successfully with every type of product and service imaginable, and it capitalizes on the fact that people will always pay more for ideas than for products.

TABLE 3.1   Criteria ranked very important for
major purchase decisions.

Criteria	Percentage
Offers the right features	83.3
Careful evaluation and comparison	75.8
Discounted or sale price	39.8
Responsiveness of sales and service people	37.5
Reviews and testimonials	37.0
Opinions of immediate family	23.0
Opinions of trusted friend	14.8

Source: APD Research Findings, June 2004 research project, *How the Affluent Make Purchasing Decisions,* commissioned by The Oechsli Institute.

Concept selling begins by learning about your prospective customer's goals and aspirations within the context of your product and service category. The crucial mistake made by my former dentist's office was not knowing their customer (patient)—me. They should have perused my file, reviewed my past x-rays, and had a better understanding of me, my teeth, and my dental goals.

When you can sell someone on the concept of a high-tech entertainment center, the exact functional features and pricing become less important. You must become a consultant who understands how to create different types of entertainment environments, even if it involves products you do not sell. Then your knowledge becomes part of the value that your customer buys, and you have established an ongoing relationship. That becomes the framework within which the seven pieces of the affluent sales environment puzzle fit and blend together to establish exactly the right sales environment for that individual.

Here are several examples of how companies and salespeople have created the type of sales environments that work for their affluent customers and for them:

- Tom sells homes in the $300,000 to $500,000 range, and he believes that his background as a human resources manager is a key reason for his success with selling in the upscale market. Tom says that learning how to listen was one of the most important lessons he learned. "They want to be assured that you are knowledgeable and have experience working with properties like the one they are selling or want to buy. You don't have to tell them how to invest their money or what kind of financing they need. You can't be pushy. This kind of customer doesn't want to be bugged. These are successful people, and they want to be treated differently."
- An office furniture retailer in California tells how they once sold furniture but have since learned the value of selling a home office concept. Carl, a VP, says that "Everybody that has

a computer at home has a home office today, even if it's a corner of a family room or a second bedroom. The woman's view is that she doesn't want that big mess sticking out and staring at her all day. When they ask for home office furniture, we can offer a multitude of choices to help them create a coordinated configuration." The store has eight designers on staff—not salespeople. Carl puts it this way, "Without a design background, they really can't do a client justice."

- For many photography consumers, portraits have become more commonplace and less of a valued experience. Most photographers try to either compete with high-volume retail store portrait studios or find their own niche in the better paying upscale market. One studio that targets the affluent uses a concept selling approach they call "life cycle selling" where they presell clients to return at their next "cycle" of life for another portrait. Typical customers make major portrait investments five to six times over the years. They become lifelong clients. When a client asks whether they have any specials, the response is, "Everything we do is special." They find that having a reputation for being expensive is the best thing that could have happened to them.

- Selling window coverings is one of those areas where the emphasis on functional areas such as durability, performance, light control, and thermal benefits has created a commodity sales environment that makes it more and more difficult to compete. Concept selling has changed all that for one dealer. The dealer begins by asking about the customer's goals and dreams for his or her home. If the client is buying new window coverings, chances are there are other things in the works—such as new flooring, furniture, and wall coverings. This dealer knows that beauty and pride in their home are important to all affluent homeowners, so the salespeople focus on selling the homeowner on the concept of a beautiful room.

While concentrating on creating the right sales environment, it's easy to forget that waiting for the affluent to walk in your door is not enough. You will need to seek every opportunity to go to them and strategically place yourself in their path, focusing on their agenda instead of your agenda, so that you do not run the risk of not connecting with your affluent prospect, customer, or patient. We discuss how to accomplish that in Chapter 5, but first in Chapter 4, we look at the common roadblock of social self-consciousness that may be keeping you from going down that path.

SUMMARY

From the incidents described in Chapter 2, we can identify 10 ways to drive affluent customers and clients away: neglect, poor quality service, complacency and inefficiency, inconvenience, technical deficiencies, being manipulative, being deceptive, telling rather than listening, using too much technical jargon, and being impersonal.

You must create an affluent sales environment that is built on seven principles: proactive relationship building, convenience, seamless selling, upscale quality, Ritz-Carlton level service, FedEx level efficiency, and integrity.

Concept selling is the heart and soul of an affluent sales environment. It begins by learning about your prospective customer's goals

---

Research Facts

➤ Having friendly and helpful people who represent the supplier (sales or service personnel) was very important to 62.5 percent of our survey respondents in determining whether they would use the same product or service provider again.

➤ Offering the lowest price available was ranked by 44.3 percent of respondents as having considerable influence on whether they would use the same product or service provider again.

---

and aspirations as they relate to your products and services. Effective conceptual selling places a premium on aesthetic value and relationships, making functional features and pricing less important.

Waiting for the affluent to walk in your door is not enough. You must seek every opportunity to place yourself in their path.

TAKING ACTION

- Take inventory of your sales environment. Using the "Ten Ways to Drive Affluent Customers Away" and the seven principles for creating an affluent sales environment as your guide, create three lists: (1) what we need to *eliminate* and *stop* doing, (2) what we need to *keep* and *continue* doing, and (3) what we need to *add* and *start* doing.
- Continue researching where the affluent "hang out" in your community, remembering that waiting for them to walk in your door isn't enough. You must place yourself in their path—and your first step is to find out where to go. You will learn exactly how to do that in Chapter 5.
- Identify what is within your immediate control that you can change within 24 hours that will improve your affluent sales environment.

4

OVERCOMING SOCIAL
SELF-CONSCIOUSNESS

Salespeople need to be confident in their ability to provide affluent prospects with everything necessary to help them make a decision suitable to their needs and wants.

—Factoid, 2004 APD Research

I am assuming that you are a sales professional whose product or service is aimed at the affluent consumer. If so, think for a moment about what you have already learned. We described the affluent opportunity and discovered that this targeted group controls approximately 89 percent of all the liquid assets in the United States.

In Chapter 2, you had an opportunity to pry open the lid and take a peek into the affluent mind. Building on that insight, Chapter 3 explained how to build the right sales environment to attract, sell, and retain the loyalty of affluent customers and clients. By now, you no doubt realize that the opportunity to sell products and services to the affluent is like manna from heaven.

Most likely, your firm has invested heavily to make certain that the products and services you sell provide the features and benefits the affluent want most. Corporate training departments are busy arming their salespeople (you) with the product knowledge and sales techniques necessary to present all the bells and whistles. Your stars are aligned, and everyone is excited—right?

Not necessarily. Become invisible and slip into the showrooms and sales offices where salespeople are being afforded this remarkable opportunity. With just a quick glance, you could easily be fooled. Although there is likely to be a lot of activity going on, someone with a more discerning eye will notice that much of what is "going on" is not proactive prospecting and selling activity. It is busy work, and some of it could be accurately described as "avoidance behavior." This is a common occurrence in every company these days, but it is especially true when the company has recently refocused everyone's efforts upscale.

Larry, a financial advisor, blessed me with three hours of personal conversation on a flight to Las Vegas. He had the gift of gab, and it did not take him long to discover that I was up to my ears in research about the affluent. I, on the other hand, was curious about how Larry was marketing himself to the affluent. What began as a series of questions from Larry to me resulted in a very fascinating flight. "I've always been intimidated by people with power and money," mused Larry. "I've tried to play the part. Heck, I drive a new 7 series BMW, wear $2,000 suits and $200 shirts. But I continue to find excuses to avoid affluent people. I don't socialize with them. I don't even belong to the local country club where all the serious money plays golf, and I know that I should," he confessed.

Larry was not only suffering from social self-consciousness but also was one of the few salespeople who are acutely aware of it and willing to talk about it. Granted, he was talking to me after learning that I had expertise in the arena of the affluent. I was fascinated as I listened to Larry's candid assessment of his expensive image. "If I'm honest," he continued, "I use the BMW and expensive clothes to impress people who are lower on the socioeconomic ladder. For some strange reason, it makes me feel good. But I just can't make any money selling my services to those people."

I asked how many new affluent clients he would like to sell his financial advisory services to over the next 12 months. After a good long silence, he replied, "Fifteen. If I could bring in 15 new $1 million relationships, I'd be giving myself a $120,000 raise." But social self-consciousness can be contagious. Larry's wife recently received her realtor's license, enabling her to sell upscale houses in their community. According to Larry, she's also intimidated by people whom she considers wealthy. He figures that he'll have to line up prospects for her, which sounds a lot like the pot calling the kettle black.

It's amazing what you can learn on a three-hour flight. Larry had previously been married to a physician. He didn't give any of the details of what went wrong, other than to indicate that he didn't seem to relate well with doctors. He met his current wife at a local restaurant that he frequented, where, in his words, "She was the gorgeous little hostess." Without going any further, it would be easy to make the inference that Larry was intimidated by his physician wife; but an attractive hostess, someone who was impressed by his BMW and $2,000 suits, made him more comfortable.

Hello, social self-consciousness! In lay sales terms, you might want to call it *affluent sales reluctance*. George Dudley and Shannon Goodson, authors of *The Psychology of Sales Call Reluctance: Earning What You're Worth* (1999), define social self-consciousness in salespeople as shunning "prospects of wealth, prestige, power, education or social standing" (p. 119). They go on to describe the negative impact it can have on an otherwise healthy sales career when a salesperson shifts his or her emphasis to up-market clients. Dudley explains the significance of social self-consciousness this way:

> One reason social self-consciousness is such a dangerous form of sales call reluctance is that it flies well under the radar of all but one sales selection test. That's because it is so highly "localized." Only one form of prospecting becomes impaired. All other forms are left unbothered. That means candidates may not be shy, timid, or even inexperienced. Their other prospecting skills may dazzle recruiters. Personality-based tests are notorious for failing to detect specific prospecting problems like social self-consciousness,

and award them scores like "highly recommend." That illusion persists only until it's time to contact prospective buyers with wealth, education, power or social standing. (p. 125)

Dudley and Goodson would also tell us that Larry's situation is not an aberration.

No one is born with social self-conscious call reluctance—it is learned—and it is highly contagious. Often it is confused with low self-esteem and low assertiveness.

Their research shows that social self-consciousness is contagious. Obviously, none of this is really important until you begin to target the affluent. Whether you or your company initiated the shift upscale is not the issue. The impact is the same. Here are the facts, backed by solid research:

- Approximately 35 percent of all salespeople across every industry struggle with social self-consciousness.
- Social self-consciousness can negatively impact your sales career even if you prospect effectively with those you do not perceive as affluent.
- The issue is not how successful a salesperson you are. The issue is the amount of emotional stress you experience when contacting, or even thinking about contacting, someone of wealth, prestige, power, education, or social standing.
- Social self-consciousness will not go away by simply saying, "Just do it!" Emphasizing positive thinking does not work. In fact, people with social self-consciousness tend to read more self-help books than the average salesperson. The studies show that all those books and tapes and seminars will not help with this issue.

Surprisingly, social self-consciousness is most common in veteran salespeople. Here is a conversation I had following a keynote speech with two financial professionals, successful 15- and 17-year veterans, respectively. We were discussing the possibilities of my coaching them, and they were particularly concerned with getting more affluent clients and with marketing and selling to the affluent. Bob was a former teacher and had a master's degree in education; Luke was a certified public accountant.

"We've had previous coaching relationships that didn't really work out," explained Bob, who was acting as the spokesperson. I gave him a puzzled look, one that said, "Am I being set up as the next coach to fail in meeting your expectations?" Reading my thoughts, he began to clarify. "We do everything extremely well. We have a very well-run practice, know how to sell, and offer a valuable service. All we need is for someone to help us find and attract more affluent prospects."

After probing further, it was clear that Bob was serious. At the same time, both Bob and Luke were in denial. The fact was, both were in daily contact with affluent prospects. Bob was a member of the wealthiest church in their area, and Luke belonged to the Rotary Club, which included every powerful person in the entire region among its members. Not only that: Both had high-profile leadership roles in their respective organizations. You could not orchestrate a better scenario!

When I laughed and suggested that it would not be fair for me to accept their money when they were already in front of affluent prospects, it was clear that they did not appreciate my humor. They were convinced that it was taboo to "sell" in these organizations. I introduced the issue of social self-consciousness and explained that I would consider a coaching relationship but that my first task would be to help them break through that barrier and capitalize on the gold mine right there in front of them. They both pushed back hard and fast. "You don't understand," explained Luke in a rather condescending tone, "in the circles we run in, if you come off as a salesperson, you're dead."

Social self-consciousness has been documented in more than 73 industries; for example, accounting, apparel, automotive, banking, cable television, club management, computers, cosmetics, electronics, financial advisors/stockbrokers, food distribution, funeral services, geriatric and residential care, hotel and hospitality, insurance, interior decorating, legal, moving and transfer, office products, pharmaceutical, printing, real estate, security systems, telecommunications, travel services, utilities, and video satellite services.

It is not difficult to envision how the affluent sales environment described in Chapter 3 could be applied to each one of these industries. If social self-consciousness impacts such a broad spectrum, you can also be confident that it is holding otherwise competent salespeople back in every other industry that is targeting the affluent. The bad news is that without proper intervention, there is an 87 percent chance that social self-consciousness will plague you throughout your sales career.

But there is also really good news. Dudley and Goodson suggest that when this form of call reluctance is detected early and the proper remedy is provided, it is relatively easy to correct. In fact, it took a bit of persuading, but Bob and Luke finally acknowledged their problem and asked me to help them.

WHAT'S REALLY HOLDING YOU BACK?

Like many financial advisors today, Bob and Luke wanted to maximize their earning potential, and they realized that they had to be selling to the affluent to accomplish that goal. Their social self-consciousness initially caused them to be in denial. Because they both associated with affluent people socially on a daily basis, neither could believe they were affected by social self-consciousness. Although the bylaws in their respective organizations forbade soliciting business, it took an honest and close inspection to uncover the fact that members of these prestigious organizations did discreetly conduct business with one another.

If you see a bit of yourself in the preceding example, you should be aware that this is not a case of low self-esteem, low goal motivation, or a lack of assertiveness. In fact, it often happens with those who are above average in all three of those characteristics except when it comes to approaching prospects of wealth, prestige, and power. Some clues that suggest that social self-consciousness may exist include:

- Setting sales goals but failing to follow through.
- Exaggerating the power, prestige, and fame of affluent individuals, both in your own thinking and verbally to others.
- Telling others, "I'm not really interested in whether my customers are affluent. There are other segments of the market."
- Feeling self-conscious and becoming tongue-tied when in the presence of affluent people.
- Trying to intimidate people at lower levels in your organization as a way of compensating for your own frustrations with feeling intimidated around wealth.

As Dudley and Goodson helpfully point out, these emotional boundaries are all self-inflicted, which means they can be overcome—with effort. The first step is to make a quick assessment to determine whether social self-consciousness might be something that is holding you back.

EVALUATING SOCIAL SELF-CONSCIOUSNESS

As with any effort to look closely at yourself, this evaluation requires both honesty and courage. Otherwise, the effort has little value.

Is social self-consciousness a problem with you? There are only two options—yes or no. So take a deep breath, read each of the statements in the table on page 65, and circle YES or NO for each statement.

The key issue is this: How large a blockage is social self-consciousness in holding you back from enthusiastically reaching your goals? To answer this question, add the number of times you circled YES: _____. Circle the number on the following continuum:

Significant Action Is Needed			Moderate Action Is Needed			NO Action Is Needed	
7	6	5	4	3	2	1	0

I cannot overemphasize the importance of being completely honest with yourself on this issue. Nobody likes to admit to a weakness, especially when it involves intimidation. As a result, there is a tendency for some sales professionals to rationalize everything, trying to convince themselves that they have no problem when they are face-to-face with an affluent prospect.

I observed an example of this rationalization when I was asked to spend time with a father-daughter wealth management team to discuss their business development efforts. The father had developed a healthy asset base. His daughter, armed with an MBA and technology savvy, was fairly new in the business. On the surface, their issue was getting the father to become more active in developing new business. "All we need to do is get more activity. Once we get prospects in our office and take them through our investment process, we close virtually 100 percent," explained the daughter, while the father nodded approvingly. When I responded, "Then obviously you are not dealing with the affluent," the daughter began to protest, but Dad waved her off and replied, "If we're honest with ourselves, we are not thinking big enough. We both need to do a better job of getting in front of affluent prospects. We know plenty of wealthy people, but we've never had the courage to discuss business with any of them."

I knew by the way they described their sales environment that they were not dealing with wealthy prospects. But only after confronting them would they admit that I was right. Both were suffering from social self-consciousness, and the daughter was still fumbling with excuses as I left. She kept saying something about having young children and not being willing to trade her family

	Is This a Problem?	
1. I have set goals that involve selling to the affluent, but I have not been able to achieve them.	YES	NO
2. When pushed, I frequently give some reason why I am not interested in pushing myself.	YES	NO
3. I often feel uneasy in the presence of people I view as having wealth, power, prestige, and fame.	YES	NO
4. I sometimes catch myself being somewhat tongue-tied when conversing with people of wealth and prestige.	YES	NO
5. I must admit that I tend to exaggerate the power, prestige, and influence of people with wealth.	YES	NO
6. There are times when I talk down to and treat people in support positions worse than I should—to make them feel the way I do around people of power and influence.	YES	NO
7. I need and want to be proactive in selling to the affluent, but I really feel stuck.	YES	NO

time for going out and getting face-to-face with affluent prospects. This was a curious objection considering she was already working close to 10 hours every working day. Remember, honesty is essential.

TAKING ACTION TO BREAK OUT
AND MOVE AHEAD

Once you determine that you suffer from social self-consciousness, your next step is to decide that you will take appropriate action to overcome any aspects of social self-consciousness that are holding you back. Following are several suggestions:

- *Preparation:*
  —Develop a list of ideal affluent prospects, and identify the sources you can tap to add to that list.
  —Determine your "value hook." What information and advice can you add to the products and services you sell so that you can become the person that affluent people want to go to for the help that they need?
- *Mental rehearsal:* Right before each face-to-face encounter, visualize exactly the results that you want. Whether you will be on the golf course, at a church committee meeting, or bumping into an affluent prospect through a carefully orchestrated coincidental meeting at your local Starbucks—if you can visualize a successful encounter in your mind, the image you create will have a positive impact on your results. Top athletes and actors have used this type of visualization or mental rehearsal for years.
- *Action:* Regardless of your preparation and visualization, your apprehension will not totally disappear. The key is to not allow those feelings of apprehension to keep you from doing what you need to do. Following are three techniques that will help you to relax, beat away the emotional demons

attempting to sabotage your efforts, and give you a better chance at performing well:

1. *Mental signal:* I have had clients experience good results by visualizing a candle flame whenever they sense doubt or feel nervous. Simply visualize a candle flame in your mind, take a deep breath, exhale slowly, and feel anxiety flush out of your system as you exhale.

2. *Rubber band:* Place a rubber band around your wrist. When you catch a negative thought or feeling entering your mind, stop it by snapping the rubber band (back of your hand, not underneath). Those negative thoughts will stop immediately.

3. *Positive affirmations:* Whenever you catch yourself having a negative thought, replace it with a positive affirmation. For example, if you're thinking, "I'm too nervous . . ." replace it with, "I'm relaxed and confident." This works especially well right after you blow out the candle flame or snap the rubber band.

These techniques work because they serve to realign your thoughts. Most, if not all, of our negative feelings and anxiety are caused by the view we take of situations, not the situations themselves. If we keep thinking about all the bad things that might happen, our body accepts those thoughts as truth because it cannot distinguish fact from fiction.

It is important at this point to beware of ego interference and pride. No one likes to admit that he or she is intimidated by someone else, especially when there doesn't seem to be a valid reason for it. But, if it exists, admit it. Then do something about it.

YOUR CONSCIOUS THOUGHT
MANAGEMENT ACTION PLAN

Becoming aware that you have a social self-consciousness problem and initiating the preceding actions may be all you need to do to get unstuck and overcome any affluent reluctance you may be experiencing. If so, that's great!

Regardless, this is not the only challenge you face. Programming your mind for success can be critically important. Everything you are today is the result of your collective thinking up to this point. Everything you will become will be the result of the content of your thoughts from this point forward.

The idea behind conscious thought management is that if you want to experience success in sales, you will dramatically increase your probability of success if you take action to concentrate on that mental picture until it becomes reality. There are four steps to your Conscious Thought Management Action Plan. The first three are very easy to implement and can and should be done each day. The fourth will take more preparation, but after that, it, too, is easy to implement.

Technique 1: Starting Out Right

During the first hour after awakening, the subconscious mind is more amenable to new programming than at any other time. As soon as you arise in the morning, say, "I feel terrific! I feel great!" Then spend 20 to 30 minutes reading something inspirational, motivational, or instructional. Do *not* listen to the news or anything that might stimulate negative thinking. We are all energy forces, and it is your responsibility to make certain that your energy is not only positive but also infectious.

Technique 2: Getting Back on Track

We all have "down times" during the day—coffee breaks, meal breaks, or traveling between calls. Those are the times that we are most susceptible to negative self-talk, especially if we have just had a negative experience with a prospect, a customer complaint, or are simply struggling with social self-consciousness. From now on, make certain that you fill every down time with listening to inspirational messages or reading that will fill your conscious mind with positive thoughts. You need more than caffeine to recharge your energy forces during the course of a day.

Technique 3: Associating with the Right People

The people that we associate with often have the greatest influence on us. So, if you are serious about becoming affluent through your sales efforts, it is important to associate with people who will positively reinforce your thoughts and efforts. This is easier said than done. Why? Although most people would love to be successful, they aren't willing to pay the price. Consequently, they are envious of anyone who they think is paying the price. This jealousy frequently takes the form of subtle sabotage with comments like, "What are you working so hard for? You already make enough money," and so on.

What this means is that you must be able to detect a jealous saboteur quickly and avoid that person like the plague. Whether it requires avoiding a new associate or adding someone new to your reference group, make your associations a choice—and choose carefully.

Technique 4: Creating a Self-Affirmation CD or Tape

Garbage in, garbage out! The best way to take heed of this warning is to replace any garbage in with a habit of daily self-affirmation. It requires initial effort to write and record a CD or tape that you can play over and over, but it will be worth it. Creating a self-affirmation CD or tape is simple. It's based on the 7-7-7 rule:

- Seven affirmation statements
- Repeated seven times each
- Spaced seven seconds apart

The most beneficial approach is to look at your total life and seek balance when creating your seven affirmation statements.

Focus on areas that you *want to change* and areas that you *don't want to neglect.*

To achieve this balance, I suggest you develop your affirmation statements including three to four statements focused on areas relating to affluent sales success and three to four statements focused on any combination of the following: physical health, mental health, spiritual, marriage, family, social, educational, personal growth.

The words you select for your affirmation statements are important. They will determine the pictures that are formed in your subconscious mind, so follow these guidelines:

- *Personal*—Begin each statement with words such as:

  I am . . . I have . . . It's easy for me to . . . I enjoy . . . I love . . .

  Do not say: My manager will praise me when I make an affluent sale.

  Say: I love selling my [services/products] to the affluent.

- *Positive*—Focus on what you ideally want in the future. Leave your problems behind:

  Do not say: I am no longer worrying about my physical health.

  Say: I am healthy and fit.

- *Present tense*—Say it as if it is true right now. This will probe your subconscious mind to act automatically as if what you are saying *is* reality:

  Do not say: I will become knowledgeable about the wealthy small business owners in our area.

  Say: I am knowledgeable about the wealthy small business owners in our area.

- *Comparison free*—Comparing yourself to others creates a false sense of reality in your mind. Commit to acquiring the qualities of the high achievers you admire, but do not compare yourself with them.

Do not say: I am going to improve my presentation to be better than Bill's.

Say: It's easy for me to develop rapport, articulate my value, and develop new affluent clients/customers.

- *Private*—Affirmations are for private use. Don't share them with anyone except a working partner who is using the same technique. People not using conscious thought management tend not to understand. Some may even try to sabotage your efforts, even though they say they are trying to help you. By keeping your affirmation statements to yourself, you will be able to say what you really want to say.

Here are three steps you can use to write each of your seven affirmation statements:

1. Think of a dimension of your life that you want to change. Write that *change area* on a piece of paper.
2. Imagine yourself in a situation where you have already made that change and are enjoying the results. Describe that *image* next.
3. Use what you imagined to guide you in writing a powerful *affirmation statement* (as shown in the box on the top of page 72).

Example

Following are samples of HNW affirmations that other salespeople have successfully used to overcome their social self-consciousness:

- I command professional respect effortlessly when I am with affluent prospects.
- I eagerly and confidently look forward to meeting with affluent prospects.

Change area: I would like to be confident with High Net Worth (HNW) prospecting.

Image: I am introduced to a HNW prospect by a HNW client. I am full of confidence and positive energy, and I make natural eye contact when shaking hands. My use of reverse psychology in suggesting that we both need to discover whether there is a fit causes the prospect to compliment my professionalism.

Affirmation statement: I am confident and able to bring high energy to each encounter with HNW prospects.

- I consistently provide high-quality, valued service to my affluent clients.
- I know how to gain the trust of affluent prospects.
- I am an affluent client-prospecting machine.
- I prospect every day for new affluent customers.
- Everywhere I go and in everything I do, I look for affluent prospecting opportunities.
- My affluent selling skills are seamless.
- I am always under control when in the presence of affluent people.
- I build rapport with affluent prospects quickly.
- I ask for affluent prospect introductions and referrals at every opportunity.
- I am totally focused on activities that enhance my affluent prospecting efforts.

An effective method for developing and getting the greatest use out of affirmations is to place each one on a 3 × 5 card. Carry those cards with you everywhere you go. You can then refer to them whenever you feel the need—and even when you don't feel the need, knowing the kind of extra energy that reviewing your affirmations can provide.

Conscious thought management is only a part of the solution. The other component is *action*. I do not know whether Larry acted on the action plan that I helped him develop. On the other hand, I can tell you it took Bob and Larry less than a month and three challenging conference calls with me to make their breakthrough. Although they were targeting different affluent centers of influence, through the combination of conscious thought management supported by specific action steps that were different for each, they were able to overcome their social self-consciousness together.

As George Dudley (personal communication, April 30, 2004) assured me in an interview I conducted while writing this chapter, "When diagnosed early, social self-consciousness is easy to correct." If you are saying, "I enjoy meeting with affluent prospects," seven times each day, you are talking the right walk. You also need to walk the talk so that your affirmation is consistent with your action. It's all about consistently doing the right things, the right way, to the right affluent people, for the right reasons.

SUMMARY

For those companies targeting the affluent today, much of the activity in their field showrooms and sales offices is busy work or, more accurately, "avoidance behavior." The culprit is what George Dudley and Shannon Goodson call *social self-consciousness.*

No one is born with social self-consciousness. It is learned, and it is highly contagious. Social self-consciousness will not go away by simply saying, "Just do it!" Nor does emphasizing positive-thinking work. When it is identified accurately and the proper remedy is provided, it is relatively easy to correct.

You probably wrestle with social self-consciousness if you set prospecting and sales goals relating to the affluent market and then fail to follow through. Other clues include feeling

> ## Research Facts
>
> ➢ Thirty-five percent of all salespeople in every industry struggle with social self-consciousness.
> ➢ Social self-consciousness has been documented in more than 73 industries.
> ➢ In all eight criteria that impact the selection of a financial coordinator, there were statistically significant gaps between what clients expected and the performance of their financial professional. We know from experience that social self-consciousness is a major contributor to allowing those gaps to exist.

uncomfortable around people of wealth and avoiding any efforts to get in their path.

Your first step is to be totally honest with yourself on this issue. Your next step is to take appropriate action to overcome any social self-consciousness that may be blocking your road to success in three phases: preparation, mental rehearsal, and action.

TAKING ACTION

- Take the Social Self-Consciousness Self-Assessment in this chapter. It will benefit you only if you are totally honest with yourself.
- Complete the *preparation* step as described in the Taking Action to Break Out and Move Ahead section.
- Practice the *mental rehearsal* step so you can begin using it immediately with each face-to-face encounter you have with the affluent in your community.
- Review the four techniques relating to the *action* steps in this chapter. Select and begin implementing those you feel will help you the most. Do not overlook Technique 4: Creating a

Self-Affirmation CD or Tape. It will take time to create those affirmations, but this technique often helps more than any of the other three.

- Go out among the affluent several times a week. Using the *mental rehearsal* step and *action* step techniques to reinforce those efforts, you will be surprised how quickly any social self-consciousness you have will become a thing of the past.

5

BECOMING ONE
WITH THE AFFLUENT

Opinions and suggestions of immediate family and trusted friends are the most important criteria in deciding where to look for major purchase suppliers.

—FACTOID, 2004 APD RESEARCH

Although he was certainly no athlete, George Plimpton spent a lifetime writing about sports based on his participation in them rather than his observations of them. He pitched to Willie Mays, boxed with Archie Moore, and performed as a Clyde Beatty-Cole Brothers Circus trapeze artist. But probably his most memorable book was *Paper Lion,* documenting his exploits with the 1963 NFL Detroit Lions. In a June 1999 interview on *TIME.com,* George Plimpton was asked if he found it hard to play football with the Lions. He responded:

> Yes, since I'm not one much for physical contact. . . . It wasn't much fun on the practice field with the Lions, and the pleasure of the research for that book was in listening to them talk intimately about the game they loved. They became great friends, and two of them, Alex Karas and John Gordy, were ushers at my wedding. But the story I got was one I couldn't have, if I had not marched onto the field and tried my best. In my big game, as the quarterback, you will remember that I lost 32 yards in four plays. Very humiliating.

George Plimpton's sports stories were unique because, before he wrote about these athletes and the games they play, he became one with them. Think very carefully about three key points Plimpton highlighted in this interview:

1. He listened to them talk intimately about the game they loved, not from a distance, but as one who participated with them.
2. He became great friends with them and especially with the two who were ushers at his wedding.
3. He clearly understood that he could not have gotten the story he did if he "had not marched onto the field and tried my best" to play their game.

If you've ever seen a photo of George Plimpton, you can imagine how he must have felt walking onto the Detroit Lions' practice field—like a skinny twig among giant trees. It took great determination to put his feelings of intimidation aside and become involved in all that physical contact. Plimpton's experience was not unlike what we explored in Chapter 4 about overcoming the feelings of intimidation caused by social self-consciousness.

Don't let the factoid at the beginning of this chapter get confused with the findings you read about in Chapter 3, where you discovered the importance of seven specific criteria in making a final major purchase decision. That is very different from the criteria that impact getting you face-to-face with a potential major purchaser. George Plimpton might have been referred to the Detroit Lions by a trusted friend, but the only way he would have been allowed to actually play on the team would be if he possessed the right skill package after a brutal tryout. In other words, his features and benefits as a football player, carefully evaluated and compared against others, would be the determining criteria, not whom George Plimpton knew. The same is true in your world, except you have a much better chance of possessing the features and benefits necessary to get the business.

Becoming one with the Lions was as far as it went for George Plimpton. He never aspired to become one of them, nor did he have the ability to make the team if he wanted to. That is not the case with you. Becoming one with the affluent will create the opportunity for you to also become one of them. Being intimately involved with the affluent will quickly turn you into one of the aspiring affluent described in Chapter 1, if you aren't one already. From there, it will only be a matter of time as your opportunities, goals, and selling activities transform your aspirations into reality. We pointed out earlier that many in the affluent and super-rich categories are businesspeople and experienced professionals. That was confirmed by our research. In fact, 44.9 percent of the respondents were corporate employees, earning their income through salary and commission. That includes salespeople. If they could achieve that level of success, so can you.

STEPPING ONTO THE PLAYING FIELD

This is where the sports allegory takes a new tack. There is no practice field for you. You need to go to the playing field where real things are happening for the affluent in your community. But don't feel discouraged. It's much easier to place yourself in their path and meet affluent prospects socially than it is to try to reach them by phone. Your goal is to become involved with them in the things that are important to them, because you definitely know by now that sitting and waiting for them to come to you is a bad choice. This goes beyond simply joining organizations. Many salespeople join the right organizations but rarely attend functions, let alone become involved with other members in important activities.

There are many organizations you can consider joining, and we will list a number of them. First, however, it is important to establish a list of criteria to use in selecting the best types of organizations for you. Here are six questions to explore:

Joining Organizations—Six Selection Criteria

1. Do the activities and events attract wealthy individuals? Some organizations have wealthy people on their rolls, but not at their functions.

2. Does this organization provide opportunities to meet new people at least monthly? That includes meetings, activities, and social events. Some organizations schedule events two to four times a year, and that is not enough.
3. Are they recognized as a gathering place for the wealthy? When you mention the organization's name, people should immediately comment on the elite membership.
4. Do their purpose and goals capture your interest? It will be difficult to stay involved if you aren't drawn in some meaningful way to what they do.
5. Are they viewed as making a positive contribution to the community? Avoid organizations that embroil themselves in controversial issues.
6. Can you afford to be involved? Go beyond basic membership fees and check the typical cost of monthly meetings, special events, and expected contributions to any fundraising activities.

There are a number of organizations that would typically meet your criteria. The most obvious ones include:

- Alumni associations
- Chambers of commerce
- Charities
- Churches, synagogues, and other religious organizations
- Civic organizations
- Clubs organized around special interests such as gourmet foods, antique cars, and wine tasting
- Country clubs
- Economic clubs
- Fraternal organizations
- Hospitals and other major medical organizations
- Museums
- Private clubs

- Professional organizations
- Rotary Club

As you explore this list and consider which organization(s) would be best for you, keep in mind that the first step affluent shoppers take when making a major purchase is to determine which suppliers to contact. When making that decision, our research clearly shows that they give the greatest credibility to the suggestions and opinions of their immediate family and trusted friends. As I stated earlier in this chapter, there is a distinct difference between what impacts the decision of which suppliers to contact and what impacts the final purchase decision.

Many a salesperson has lost business because he or she failed to make this distinction. Getting a quality referral or introduction is great, but assuming that a referred affluent prospect is going to conduct business with you because of this referral is foolish. Because you know it has very little impact on the final decision, you will then proceed carefully to uncover exactly what prospects want, all the bells and whistles included. From there you can guide them in making their decision to conduct business with you.

In Chapter 7, we discuss the importance of "becoming magnetic" in your prospecting efforts. As we emphasize there, that process actually begins here. Selecting the organization(s) that will be best for you is your first step toward becoming that trusted friend that affluent members go to, especially when it comes to the products and services you offer.

The key is to narrow down your list and focus. To further explore how you can place yourself in the path of the affluent people you want to reach, write your answers to the following questions on a legal pad:

- Who are the five prime affluent people in my community that I want to meet?
- What upcoming events might those five people attend?

- What watering holes do those five people frequent?
- What causes do those five people support?
- Based on my answers to these questions, what three specific organizations from the preceding list should I investigate and possibly join?

After you determine where you should become involved, the question is how and when. Start by making a list of meetings and events you will attend and entering them into your day planner. But don't simply "attend." Preparation for each is vital to your success. Here is what you should do:

Event Preparation Checklist

1. *Plan your involvement.* Determine who will be there, what your networking objectives will be, and what you need to take.
2. *Show up early.* Arrive ready to network, and stop at the entrance to plan your first move.
3. *Walk the room at least twice.* Become familiar with the area and who is there, especially if the event is held in a large room.
4. *Stay alert.* Eat early, don't drink, and don't smoke.
5. *Spend at least 75 percent of your time with people you don't know.* Resist the temptation to escape with someone you know.
6. *Target those you want to meet.* Identify three to six people.
7. *Approach, smile, and shake hands firmly.* Show warmth and display confidence.
8. *Say people's names at least twice.* First, it helps you remember their names. Second, a person's name is the most pleasing word to his or her ears.
9. *Tell others your name and what you do.* But be brief. Help them help you by giving them only enough to encourage them to ask questions.

10. *Exchange cards, if it is appropriate.* Ask for the person's card, but give your card only if he or she asks for it.

11. *Ask others something to get them talking about themselves.* At any event, ask, "What brings you here tonight (today)?" At a meeting, ask something about a noncontroversial agenda item.

12. *Keep asking questions to get others to tell you more about themselves.* Keep probing so you can begin developing a relationship based on what they enjoy most—talking about themselves.

STEPPING OUTSIDE THE BOX

Joining these organizations to become involved with the affluent of your community certainly puts you on the same playing field with them. But there are also ways you can step outside the box and, in a sense, become one with the affluent by drawing targeted affluent prospects to your playing field. Here are two examples.

Joel was an interior decorator in a medium-size market of approximately one million in population. He faced tremendous competition. Affluent homeowners could choose from numerous interior decorators, but in spite of that, Joel became known as *the* interior decorator to the affluent. He was scheduled three to four months in advance and charged $350 per hour—a significantly higher rate than all of his competitors.

Even though Joel was a member of the chamber of commerce and was involved in a local charity with affluent people, that was not his primary strategy for achieving elite status. But before I divulge his unique strategy, it's important to emphasize that Joel had a creative and tasteful flair and was very good at what he did. Joel's strategy was to purchase a large home in a fashionable historic neighborhood and then turn his home into a designer showcase for his business. Each room had a different theme, which he would change whenever he felt the time was right. His office was out of the way on the third floor.

Every year, Joel invited the "who's who" in money and influence to a first-class bash at his home. It started small but quickly built as the word spread. People attended not only to see what Joel considered to be the upcoming trends in room design and furniture but also to be seen and to do their own networking. They wore everything from tuxedos and gowns to casual attire. It was a risky investment at first, but there was no doubt that Joel had successfully used this annual event to become one with the affluent by having them become one with him.

Ted was a realtor who also targeted the affluent. He was a very active chamber of commerce member and would frequently be seen entertaining a client or prospect at the City Club, a business membership dinner club. Ted was also present at every Arts Council fund-raiser. But what really set Ted apart from other realtors was his unique brand of open house: Anyone who listed a home with Ted was treated to a catered open house. It wasn't as extravagant as Joel's annual bash, but it created a warm, homelike atmosphere that attracted people of wealth. In addition to traditional advertising, Ted sent invitations to everyone in his database to help create traffic. Even though some who attended weren't currently in the market for a home, it became a mini-social event that produced a word-of-mouth network that often resulted in potential buyers that Ted could not have otherwise tapped. While his competitors were making snide comments about these events, Ted was becoming established as the preferred realtor of the affluent.

Joel had little in common with his clientele other than his professional expertise. It was his foresight in transforming a large historic house into what might be described as a "living" brochure, coupled with the courage and affluent sales acumen and ability to showcase his living brochure to the entire affluent community by holding a gala event each year that enabled Joel to quickly become "one" with the affluent community. They became his friends. The law of reciprocity was also activated, and Joel was invited to virtually every party held by anyone of substance.

Ted knew real estate, was a hard worker, and was well liked. Most important, people discovered that he could be trusted to move expensive real estate.

If we did not grow up wealthy, we tend to develop a lot of pre-conceived notions about the affluent. From the descriptions in Chapter 1, you realize that affluent people come from many different backgrounds and experiences. George Plimpton probably had some preconceived ideas about NFL football players that he later found weren't true. He didn't play football long enough to love the game as they did, but playing it with them and listening to them talk about it enabled him to better understand their world. That led to friendships that he carried with him all his life. Becoming one with the affluent, as this chapter describes, will provide the same benefits for you.

SUMMARY

George Plimpton became one with the athletes he wrote about because he listened to them talk intimately about the game they loved, became great friends with some, and clearly understood that he could not have told their story if he "had not marched onto the field and tried my best" to play their game.

There is no practice field for you, so you need to go right to the playing field where real things are happening for the affluent in your community. Your goal is to become involved with them in the things that are important to them.

There are a variety of organizations you can join—we list 14 types. Use the six criteria in this chapter to make certain that the ones you select are a gathering place for the wealthy and provide the right opportunity for you to become involved with them.

Who are the five prime affluent people in your community that you want to meet? The answer to that question can also help you select the right organization(s) for you.

Be creative! Step outside the box as Joel and Ted did.

Research Facts

➤ Of the respondents to our survey, 44 percent were corporate employees earning their income through salary and commissions, including salespeople.

➤ Our research shows that affluent buyers give the greatest credibility to the suggestions and opinions of the immediate family and trusted friends when taking that first step of determining which suppliers to contact.

➤ Our research shows, however, that opinions of immediate family and trusted friends have minimal impact on the final major purchase decision.

TAKING ACTION

- Complete your research by the end of *this* week—and then join one organization no later than *Friday.*
- Spend *next* week exploring the various ways that you can become involved as a new member. Select one of those opportunities and sign up no later than *Friday.*
- Also *next* week, select the first event you will attend. Register for it no later than *Friday.*
- Use the 12-item checklist in this chapter to prepare for any meetings or events you attend.
- Revisit your past 25 referrals and find out, if it wasn't with you, where they made their purchase and why.

6

AFFLUENT FINISHING SCHOOL

Affluent consumers are highly educated and savvy, and they are attracted to knowledgeable and professional salespeople.

—FACTOID, 2004 APD RESEARCH

Whether you are participating in a meeting at the chamber of commerce, attending a function at the country club, or helping an affluent customer with a major purchase decision, each places you face-to-face with someone you need to influence. The common thread is *face-to-face.* That's your goal. It's your critical path to affluent sales success.

As you have already discovered from our 2004 APD Research on the affluent buying decision-making process, word-of-mouth exerts the strongest influence on the affluent when they are deciding where to look for the products and services they want, and especially when a major purchase is involved. The opinions and suggestions of immediate family and trusted friends are at the top of their list. What might appear as a slap in the face is the fact that advice and recommendations of salespeople are at the bottom. This should come as no surprise. The affluent know that you know they have money. That's why they are suspicious of salespeople. The message is clear. You must be able to establish relationships through face-to-face encounters in situations where you can step outside your salesperson role, yet you must remain sales savvy at all times. It all begins with the image you project. The sole objective of this chapter is to help you improve your effectiveness in those situations.

Adam, a certified public accountant, resisted the whole idea of paying attention to his image. When I questioned him about his thoughts on the subject, his reply spoke volumes: "I'm smart. I'm honest. And I'm both a CPA and a certified financial planner. People use my services because of the knowledge and skill I bring to them, not because of the image I project." Essentially Adam was telling me that this is not a topic worthy of discussion, much less any personal effort that might be required. He recognized the fact that people did not want a slick salesperson handling their financial affairs, but he assumed that his knowledge and abilities would win the day.

Theoretically, Adam is correct. However, reality and theory are often miles apart. In Adam's case, if he had affluent clients and prospects lined up at his door because of his reputation as a CPA/financial planner, his argument would have been validated. But he didn't. The fact that he was talking to me during one of my High Net Worth Selling workshops suggested that he might not be attracting as many affluent clients as he wanted, so I took the opportunity to ask him a few performance-specific questions. I inquired about his success in selling his professional services to the affluent.

"I'm really struggling," he confessed. "In fact, if I'm really honest with you, I can barely pay my bills. I've never been very good at selling my services, and that's why I'm attending your workshop."

After the workshop, I sat down with Adam and probed further. I wanted to know what made him tick, what his clients saw, and what type of presence he was making with the affluent in his community. Within a few moments, I discovered that Adam was struggling with social self-consciousness and was using his continual quest for knowledge as a smoke screen to avoid the problem. He had become a professional student. Currently, he was working on his certified financial analyst (CFA) designation. Adam was trying to convince himself that all this image stuff was what some professionals used to mask their lack of the requisite knowledge. The mind's ability to rationalize is truly amazing! Before I go any further, let me create a word picture.

Adam wore a rumpled dark blue suit, a white button-down wash-and-wear shirt, a nondescript tie, and a pair of scuffed-up cordovan penny loafers. His handshake was soft and his eye contact poor (he kept looking down at the floor). He was fairly soft-spoken, but his vocabulary was quite good as you might expect. When I asked Adam to describe his office, his immediate response was, "It's like a rat's nest." What immediately came to my mind was a big mess with stacks of papers piled everywhere. I know I'm not being fair to Adam by asking you this. But from what you have just discovered about him, would you entrust your financial affairs to him? Guess what I was thinking at that moment.

I hoped that Adam would be able to put into action what he learned in the workshop. If he does, he will take his first step toward becoming affluent. His five-year goal was to bring in $1 million in fees a year. The other things he learned in that workshop will help him, but he first needs a complete physical makeover of both himself and his office. That outward makeover will also help him begin the inward makeover that he needs to address his social self-consciousness problem and to execute the other strategies and tactics he has learned.

I helped him make a list of purchases: two wool suits, six cotton dress shirts, five new ties, and a pair of black, all-leather tie shoes. Adam figured this new wardrobe would cost him between $750 and $1,000 at the outlet stores, which he finally admitted would be money well spent. He also agreed to hire an office organizational consultant for two hours ($75 per hour) and clean up his office. To work on the inner transformation and gain more confidence, I encouraged him to join a Dale Carnegie group in his area. Wow! All Adam thought he needed to work on was learning how to prospect and close sales.

Face-to-face communication is given strong emphasis in this chapter, in fact, in this entire book, for two reasons. First, it is the *richest* medium of communication possible. It engages all five senses and includes everything about your appearance, mannerisms, and speech matters. Second, face-to-face communication is becoming a lost art as we place increasing emphasis on the technology and techniques of telecommunication. That's why you have enrolled in this affluent finishing school.

When preparing for face-to-face meetings, as a general rule we typically focus on language. Adam was convinced that if he could get those words and phrases just right to showcase his knowledge, he would be communicating effectively. What he failed to recognize was that he was only about 7 percent correct. Why? Because 93 percent of our communication is divided between how we sound (38 percent) and how we look (55 percent). It's known as nonverbal communication, an area to which Adam had previously paid little attention. Your face-to-face encounters with affluent prospects allow for considerable nonverbal expression:

- Facial expression and eye movement
- Body language and posture
- Your physical appearance, including how you dress
- The physical distance between you and the other person
- The way you respond by nodding your head and other gestures
- Short utterances such as "okay," "yes," or "aha"
- Hand movements used to point or express action

This list suggests that there is a lot going on, and there is. But we use all those nonverbal cues without thinking, and others absorb them without even realizing it. Most people like communicating so much that they are capable of creating over 10,000 different facial expressions, for example, a single nod of the head to indicate you understand or underlining points by raising your eyebrows or pursing your lips.

Because we can all lip-read to some extent, we typically spend 75 percent of the time watching the other person speak. That's a scary thought, is it not?

MASTERING THE FIRST THREE MINUTES

At the beginning of this chapter, I mentioned three types of encounters that you are likely to have with the affluent: a business
meeting, a social event, and a sales situation. Each provides a different kind of opportunity, but all three require a face-to-face encounter in order to achieve your objectives. In each case, the first
three minutes of that encounter are critical. It took me less than 60
seconds to create a fairly accurate perception of the real Adam that
was lurking behind his credentials.

The first thing to remember is—smile! There is nothing that
makes a greater emotional impact. Research shows that the muscu-
lar action of smiling releases serotonin, a chemical in the brain for
keeping us happy. A genuine smile of enjoyment makes not only
you but also those around you feel good. It starts with your eyes.

To make a good first impression:

- Smile! Think of something pleasant, and then start smiling
  from your eyes. Relax your face and make it natural.
- Place anything you are carrying in your left hand, so you
  don't have to juggle anything to shake hands.
- Extend your right hand naturally and begin a firm (but not
  viselike) handshake.
- Prepare a self-introduction ahead of time. It should include
  your name and a tag line that quickly gives a reference point.
  See examples in the following section.

HOW TO INTRODUCE YOURSELF

Deep down, I suspect that most people think, "How do I start a
conversation with a stranger and an affluent one at that?" It's not
difficult. If you introduce yourself effectively, the conversation
will flow naturally from there.

The purpose of your introduction is to help the other person
remember your name and, if possible, give a reference point that

will create a sense of familiarity that will help him or her remember you. Connection creates comfort.

You will want to use different self-introductions for different situations, for example:

- If you are aware of a personal connection: "Hello, I'm John Doe, your fellow Yale graduate from back in '95."—or—"Hello, I'm John Doe. We live right down the street from you on Woodward Lane."—or—"Hello, I'm John Doe. I believe we frequent the same coffee shop. I often see you there on Wednesday mornings."
- If you were referred to that person: "Hi, I'm John Doe, a mutual friend of Karen Long."
- If you are active in the organization holding the meeting or event: "Hi, I'm John Doe. I serve on the chamber's promotion committee."
- If you are in a sales situation: "Welcome, I'm John Doe. I'm here to help you (state how he or she will benefit from what you do)."

Make certain that you do not make Adam's mistake of leading with your credentials. Affluent people do not care about how much you know until they become comfortable with you personally. You will initially impress them by who you are, not by how smart, talented, educated, or experienced you tell them you are.

PROJECTING THE RIGHT IMAGE

Image is primarily an attitude. If you "dress right" and "feel wrong," the negative will break through and create an image you do not want to create. That's a big part of why you should become one with the affluent. You can't sell effectively to the affluent from the sidelines. You need to move beyond believing that the affluent are bigger than life or that you need them a lot more than they need you. The relationship you seek is one where you need them *and* they need you.

Projecting the right image means appearing as those around you appear. It begins with physical appearance. Here are some important tips:

- If you're not sure whether to wear a suit, wear a suit. You can always take off your coat, and even your tie, and place them on the back of your chair.

- Dark blue tends to inspire trust on a subconscious level. Black tends to project an air of authority and is rarely a good choice for a first encounter. Adam was one of the few people attending my workshop wearing a suit. Yet, because his suit was poorly kept and his dress shirt wasn't pressed, he looked sloppy. The other attendees were dressed business casual, the dress code for the event, and presented a much better image.

- Whatever you wear, make certain that it is clean, pressed, and has no frayed cuffs or collars.

- Beards, mustaches, and dark glasses subconsciously elicit a feeling of distrust for many people—so take your shades off and be very careful in the grooming of all facial hair.

- High-quality wool material, leather belts, and leather hard-soled shoes often create the impression that you handle important matters and lucrative business transactions. I hate to keep piling on Adam, but his unshined shoes served only to highlight his poor appearance. I couldn't even tell whether they were leather. At the very least, make certain that your shoes are polished.

- If you are a female, avoid a girlish or collegiate look and hairstyle or any sexually suggestive attire.

- Avoid wearing several different colors together. It tends to diminish your professional image.
- Avoid excessive jewelry that draws attention to you (e.g., large rings, gold bracelets, large and expensive watches).

THE PYGMALION EFFECT

In classical Greek mythology, Pygmalion was a sculptor who hated women but fell in love with a statue he made of a woman. According to the myth, Pygmalion prayed to Venus, the goddess of love and beauty, to find a woman like the statue. Instead, Venus made the statue come to life.

Today, most people are familiar with the term *Pygmalion* from George Bernard Shaw's play of the same name. Adopting the same theme, a professor resurrects a girl from the streets and trains her to walk, talk, and think like a lady. As this transformation occurs, the professor falls in love with her. The play was the basis for the musical *My Fair Lady*. It was from these roots that the terms *Pygmalion effect* and *self-fulfilling prophecy* emerged.

In his classic article in the January 2003 *Harvard Business Review,* "Pygmalion in Management," J. Sterling Livingston borrowed this quote from Shaw:

> "You see," says Eliza, . . . "the difference between a lady and a flower girl is not how she behaves, but how she is treated. I shall always be a flower girl to Professor Higgins, because he always treated me as a flower girl and always will; but I know I can be a lady to you, because you always treat me as a lady and always will." (p. 97)

The Pygmalion effect is essentially the art of teaching yourself to act and dress like the person you want to become, then believing in and acting on your newfound abilities. Eliza explained the effect of self-fulfilling prophecy, whether it is good or bad. The message is this: People can be transformed, positively or negatively, into an image others create—or into the image that they create for themselves.

SELF-IMAGE FAUX PAS

A common mistake when trying to project the right image is trying too hard to impress the other person, for example:

- Talking too often and too long. Unfortunately, this becomes your discussion about you, which is the last topic an affluent prospect wants to hear about.
- Being too friendly and getting too personal. This often takes the form of using the person's nickname, slipping in a swear word, telling an off-color joke, gently delivering a light punch to the shoulder, and similar actions.
- Acting too confident and expressing assumptions that you haven't validated as yet.
- Dressing too flashy. Your clothes and jewelry should not draw attention. They should be understated, embody total professionalism, and have a subtle aura of class.

These quickly become habits that you perform without thinking. Ask people whether they notice you doing anything on the preceding list or anything else that they believe you should consider not doing. Write those actions down, and under each write what you can specifically do to replace that bad habit. The fastest way to get rid of a bad habit is to replace it with an action that creates the image and results that you want.

SPEAKING THE RIGHT MESSAGE

We've emphasized nonverbal cues, but language is also important, especially the subtle messages you send. If you are concerned about your ability to sustain a fluid conversation, locate and join a local Toastmasters' group (remember Adam). I've known many sales professionals who have benefited greatly from Toastmasters' meetings and events. Give special attention to impromptu speeches where you have to think on your feet. Another option is to hire a speech coach (your local college speech department is a good source). Here's a checklist of what should characterize your speaking habits:

- Make certain your vocabulary is fluid and absent of technical terms.
- Control your verbal content. Avoid talking about politics, religion, and controversial topics.
- Don't bad-mouth anyone, especially people from your firm and your competition.
- Maintain confidentiality at all times. If you tell "stories," change names and make certain that whatever you say would make it impossible for anyone to identify people and real situations.
- Beware (as stated before) of being too talkative. Ask questions and listen before speaking.

Everything and everyone associated with your business matters when it comes to the professional image you are striving to create and maintain in the mind of your affluent customers, clients, centers-of-influence, and prospects. Margaret, who has a rare specialty, is a case in point. She is an official divorce mediator and certified divorce planner, and she heads a professional practice that handles the financial affairs for well-heeled divorced women. Current clients and divorce attorneys in her metropolitan area are her primary centers-of-influence. Margaret has worked extremely hard to build her professionalism and her brand and to cultivate influential divorce attorneys to advocate for her.

To raise her professionalism another notch, Margaret hired a practice manager away from another firm. In Margaret's words, "Peggy is sharp as a tack. She understands this business, can multitask, and dresses like she came out of a woman's dress-for-success book. She's perfect!" Although Peggy possesses all of the qualities Margaret described, she is not perfect. Two months after joining the practice, Peggy agreed to enroll in a type of "finishing school."

The need emerged at one of the networking events Margaret and Peggy were attending. Peggy was introduced to a number of attorneys that they worked with and was then left on her own while Margaret worked the rest of the room. It was the perfect networking tactic for the team. However, a later comment from an attorney left Margaret's head spinning. After complimenting Peggy's neat appearance, he told Margaret that the slang in Peggy's speech kept distracting both him and others in the group. He mentioned noticing the subtle raised eyebrows whenever it happened (which was often). Ouch! Although spoken words account for only 7 percent of overall communication, they have the power to either reinforce or tarnish the image.

This incident forced Margaret to have a very delicate conversation with Peggy. Fortunately, Margaret had enrolled in a media school to work on her diction about five years earlier, so she was able to begin with a personal example and then advise the same route for Peggy.

If you aren't certain about your polish in any aspect of your image, find a colleague who will be open and honest with you. Ask the tough questions, and make certain that you are dissected from every angle: dress, confidence, personal energy, verbal communication, body language, manners, and anything else that you believe will help you. Remember, everything counts.

BACK TO BASICS

First published in 1937, Dale Carnegie's *How to Win Friends and Influence People* remains at the top of the list when it comes to people skills. Read it if you haven't. Reread it if you have. You will find an updated version on both the Amazon and Barnes & Noble web sites. Meanwhile, use the following to become the kind of person that everyone likes:

Dale Carnegie's Six Ways to Make People Like You

1. Become genuinely interested in other people.
2. Smile.
3. Remember that a person's name is to that person the sweetest and most important sound in any language.
4. Be a good listener. Encourage others to talk about themselves.
5. Talk in terms of the other person's interest.
7. Make the other person feel important—and do it sincerely.
8. If it hasn't sunk in yet, the material in this chapter and Chapter 5 will force you to step off the treadmill and take the necessary time to build meaningful relationships with people who can seriously impact your professional life and most likely enrich your personal life as well.

SUMMARY

A face-to-face encounter with the affluent people you want to influence is your critical path to affluent sales success. Face-to-face is the richest medium of communication possible, and it is becoming a lost art in this age of telecommunication.

Adam, a talented CPA, wore a rumpled dark blue suit, a white button-down wash-and-wear shirt, a nondescript tie, and a pair of scuffed-up cordovan penny loafers. That was not the image he needed to create when meeting face-to-face with affluent prospects.

Your face-to-face encounters allow for considerable nonverbal expression: facial expressions, eye movement, body language, physical appearance, physical distance, how you physically respond, short utterances, and hand movements.

To make a good first impression, make certain you are well prepared for the first three minutes. Use different self-introductions for different situations.

Remember the Pygmalion effect. Act and dress like the affluent person you want to become. Then believe in and act on your newfound abilities.

Research Facts

➤ Our research verifies that word-of-mouth exerts the strongest influence on the affluent when they are deciding where to look for the products and services they want, especially when a major purchase is involved.

➤ Ninety-three percent of our communication is divided between how we sound (38 percent) and how we look (55 percent).

Don't try too hard to impress people by talking too often or too long, becoming too friendly or personal, acting overconfident, or dressing too flashy.

Speak the right message. Avoid talking about controversial topics. Don't "bad-mouth" anyone. Maintain confidentiality. Beware of being too talkative. To encourage people to like you, do it the Dale Carnegie way.

TAKING ACTION

- Ask a friend or colleague to observe you during conversations with prospects or customers or clients, especially those who are affluent. Ask him or her to note and then tell you about any nonverbal cues you should correct. Write them down and review them each morning. After 30 days, ask the friend or colleague to observe you again and provide you with feedback. Continue this process until you feel that you have your body language under control.

- Make a checklist to help you prepare for appointments with prospects and customers or clients. Use the Mastering the First Three Minutes, How to Introduce Yourself, and Projecting the Right Image sections from this chapter to guide you.

- Review the Speaking the Right Message section and determine whether you would benefit from joining a Toastmasters' group.

7

BECOMING MAGNETIC

In the affluent world, because the salesperson is the product, he or she has a major impact on making or breaking the sale.

—FACTOID, 2004 APD RESEARCH

Writer Joan Popek (January 23, 2003) tells a wonderful story about how her hometown of Roswell, New Mexico, became magnetic:

> The year I turned thirteen, my mother declared that a magnet was planted in the middle of Second and Main Streets in Roswell, and everyone who passed over it would forever feel its gentle tug beckoning them home. She confessed that the rolling hills of Kansas, the cascading snows of Michigan, and the magnificent deserts of Arizona were all wonderful, but we could have all that and more if we went home to Roswell. So home we came.

That's precisely what your affluent prospects need to feel: a gentle and irresistible tug beckoning them toward what you can offer them. Our 2004 APD Research respondents validate this premise by the fact that the majority decide where to begin their search for major purchase options by listening to opinions and suggestions of immediate family members and trusted friends. And when it comes to banking, reputation for high-quality service was the most important in determining the selection process. That's the kind of magnet you need to create.

The first six chapters of this book laid the foundation. Having discovered the incredible affluent opportunity, you have probed the mind of the affluent and learned how to create the right sales environment. If social self-consciousness once held you back, it is now in your past and you are on your way toward becoming one with the affluent. To top it all off, you earned your diploma from the Affluent Finishing School. As with everything else you have learned in this book, becoming magnetic depends far more on what you *do* than on who you are and what you know. Attracting affluent prospects is the first thing you have to do.

ATTRACTING AFFLUENT PROSPECTS

There are times when affluent prospects will be searching for what you offer and, in the process, will simply find you. "Stumble upon you" is probably a better description, and in a constantly changing and fiercely competitive business environment, you cannot afford to simply wait for that to happen. You must become magnetic by finding ways to attract affluent prospects to you, and those efforts need to be characterized by the following:

- Attracting affluent prospects is a *high priority.* You never wait until you're desperate or don't have anything "better" to do.
- Rather than mass mailings, national advertising campaigns, or simply cold calling, you concentrate on the *power of networking* and *word-of-mouth-influence* to achieve your prospecting goals. As emphasized in previous chapters, the opinions and suggestions of immediate family and trusted friends are the strongest influencers when affluent buyers begin their search for the products and services they need and want. When deciding where to look for products and services, our research revealed that affluent buyers give these sources greater credibility than the information they find when searching through select periodicals or the Internet.
- Prospecting is a *planned activity.* At the beginning of each week, you define the number of new affluent contacts you must make that week, and you schedule prospecting activity each and every day.

Since you are already out among the affluent and working diligently to become one with them, you are able to capitalize on the power of networking and word-of-mouth influence. Think of the advantage that gives you over your competition. The examples provided in Chapter 2 are not isolated incidents. Most people who sell to the affluent simply wait for their company's advertising and marketing efforts to draw prospects to them. However, you also recognize that not every affluent person you meet through networking and word-of-mouth influence has a need or desire right now for what you offer. So how do you separate qualified prospects from all the others?

You don't want to come across as a salesperson, so simply telling anyone who will listen about your great products and services is the worst thing you can do. You instead want to attract affluent people who are *qualified* prospects, which essentially means that they are experiencing and feeling *dissatisfaction* about something that you can fix. Dissatisfaction can occur in at least six areas.

Six Areas of Dissatisfaction

1. They have *unfulfilled goals and aspirations* plus the desire to do something about it soon (now is even better).
2. They are *early adopters* who like to be among the first to try something new.
3. They have a *problem* that they want solved.
4. They have an *opportunity* they want to pursue.
5. *Products and/or services* they are currently using are not meeting their needs or their standards.
6. A *company, brand, and/or salesperson* they once trusted is not meeting their needs or their standards.

This last area points to the dissatisfaction that occurs following a purchase, especially one that required a major investment. One source of that dissatisfaction is the phenomenon called "buyer's remorse," which frequently occurs immediately following a major purchase. It goes something like this. Grant and Jennifer are driving their brand new car out of the dealer's parking lot, and as they head toward home, they begin to see all those other cars that look a lot like theirs—same model, same year, and even the same color. They start talking. "Our new car isn't so unique after all. Did we make the right decision? Can we afford it? Is this really the right time? Should we have waited? What if this happens? What if that happens?" As anxiety and stress begin to set in, they shift their discussion to reviewing all the reasons they made this purchase, and slowly but surely, buyer's remorse begins to diminish. However, there is also something you can do to ease this buyer's remorse. Our 2004 APD Research cites postpurchase service as one of the top two criteria that impact repeat business. If Grant and Jennifer's salesperson understood the importance of postpurchase service, he or she would take the lead and not rely on the service department.

Naturally, the real issue is whether Grant and Jennifer would return to the same salesperson at the same automobile dealer the next time they want to buy a new car. Our research points out that if either the salesperson or the dealer provided all the information Grant and Jennifer needed to make a satisfactory purchase decision, they would be more likely to return to that salesperson and dealer.

Our 2004 APD Research also identified two criteria that would have an even greater impact: (1) whether any problems they encountered following the purchase were resolved quickly and satisfactorily and (2) whether they received good service following the purchase.

The point of sale decision is soon forgotten, but the postpurchase experience looms large. Ask a few questions about that experience, and if it was negative, you will frequently find the affluent are willing, if not eager, to find a new supplier.

It's important to clearly understand the link between the products and service you offer and the dissatisfaction that affluent people might be experiencing in each of the six areas listed earlier. You can do that by creating a *product and service profile* that details the following for each product and service you offer:

- *Features:* Describe in detail what the specific features of those products and services are and what each feature does.

- *Advantages:* Detail the advantages that your product and service features have over both competitive and alternative offerings. For example, if you sell top-of-the line digital cameras, you would need to explain the advantages your models have over competitive models plus the advantages they have over using a scanner or one of the many commercial processing options available. If you have recently upgraded your product or service, explain the advantages that the new model or service has over the old. And don't forget to include the advantages of your product or service information and postpurchase service.

- *Solutions:* Don't simply list general benefits. Describe specific solutions that your products and services can provide for as many specific situations as come to mind. Don't limit yourself to specific solutions you have provided for customers/clients. That comes next.

- *Evidence:* Include any illustrations of how you have specifically provided those solutions for customers/clients. Continue to add to those illustrations with each sale you make. And again, don't overlook postpurchase service.

It's important to remember that affluent people typically do not look to salespeople to make the link between products and services offered and any possible sources of dissatisfaction. They mainly depend on three sources:

1. Friends, family, colleagues, and acquaintances whose opinions they trust
2. Reputation
3. Personal research, which is increasingly done on the Internet

You will attract affluent prospects by placing yourself in their path in such a way that they are immediately drawn to you and to what you offer. In the next chapter, we explore how to do that on the Internet, but at this point we begin where you should begin. Introductions and referrals through friends, family, colleagues, and acquaintances create the strongest attraction that you can have.

INTRODUCTIONS AND REFERRALS

Remember that you are not simply searching for people with money to spend. Instead, you want to attract affluent people who fit into one of the six dissatisfaction categories described earlier. If possible, you would like to be introduced to them. If that isn't possible, a referral is your second choice. The best people to provide those introductions and referrals are those most familiar with what you offer—your present loyal customers or clients. Second are those individuals you are getting to know at the chamber of commerce, country club, church, fraternal organizations, or wherever you have become involved in order to make those contacts. Focus on those who not only know you but also know what you do. How do you get those introductions and referrals? You ask for them. Here's an example:

> As you know, my business is built primarily through word of mouth. You have been a customer [client, colleague, fellow committee member, friend] for some time, so you have a good understanding of what I can offer. Do you know of anyone who is in need of or is interested in the benefits I can provide?

If your contact says he or she knows someone interested, continue with:

> Is there any way we could arrange a convenient introduction?

If an introduction does not seem probable:

> Would you be agreeable to my using your name when I call for an appointment?

If your contact agrees and if you believe it's appropriate:

Would you be willing to contact [him or her] in advance to let [him or her] know you have given me [his or her] name—and explain some of the ways you feel [he or she] might benefit from meeting with me?

The last sentence of the first section of this script says, "Do you know of anyone who . . ." The question concludes with ". . . the benefits I can provide?" You can be as specific here about the benefits as you wish. For example:

- *Unfilled goals and aspirations:* "someone who is eager to [fill in the blank]."
- *Early adopters:* "someone who would like to be first in line for [fill in the blank]."
- *Problem the person wants solved:* "someone who is having problems with [fill in the blank]."
- *Opportunity he or she wants to pursue:* "someone who wants to go after [fill in the blank]."
- *Products and/or services not meeting his or her needs:* "someone who is dissatisfied with [fill in the blank]."
- *A company, brand, and/or salesperson not up to his or her standards:* "someone who was disappointed by [fill in the blank]."

Establishing trust with affluent prospects is critical. Introductions and referrals create the kind of link that accelerates the trust-building process.

SEMINARS AND WORKSHOPS

Two estate-planning attorneys I know have found that providing the right seminars for the right people has enabled them to become magnetic in their own unique ways.

Jerry conducts a free three-hour seminar every month for affluent people to help them understand the value and timing issues related to estate planning. What began as an evening class at a community college has evolved into this targeted seminar because Jerry realized that by providing information free of any sales pitch, the people he wanted to reach became convinced of his integrity and sincerity. Also, the more his clients understood about estate planning when they asked for help, the better clients they became. Jerry doesn't solve individual estate issues during the workshop, but he does provide enough information for attendees to determine whether their current estate plan (if they have one) is adequate. The odds are on his side, because most estate plans were developed by attorneys who do not specialize in estate planning.

Harry, who is also an estate-planning attorney, takes a different approach. Although he works only with an affluent clientele, all of his business comes through referrals from financial advisors and financial planners. Therefore, Harry considers those financial professionals who continually refer business to him to be his first-tier clients.

To position himself as a go-to attorney for complex estate work, Harry conducts workshops at local association meetings, statewide events, national meetings, and even for a couple of major financial services companies. As far as Harry is concerned, conducting a workshop at a national meeting is a good use of his time because he is educating financial professionals to be more "judicious" in selecting who they use for their clients. He knows that anyone who, in Harry's words, "has earned a JD degree and then gets some estate-planning software can develop an estate plan and charge $5,000." So part of his mission, both locally and nationally, is to educate his clients (financial professionals) on some of the more basic intricacies of complex estate planning. He even teaches them which red flags to look for in estate plans that have already been done.

In his own market, Harry offers an open invitation to any financial professional interested in learning more about estate issues. He even gets them to buy lunch! He has positioned himself to be both the affluent client's advocate and the financial professional's strategic resource. That has made Harry truly magnetic. One hundred percent of his business comes from introductions and referrals from professionals within the financial services industry.

MIXING AND SOCIALIZING

Once you are out among the affluent and becoming one with them, you will have untold opportunities to mix and socialize. We stressed in Chapter 5 that preparation is vital to your success and gave you 12 things you should do. Every contact should be viewed as a possibility, not necessarily to buy something, but as a place to begin the process of becoming magnetic. You won't do that by talking. Asking the right question and then listening carefully in order to ask other questions is the key to your success.

It has been said that, "You can tell whether a man is clever by his answers. You can tell whether a man is wise by his questions." The benefits of becoming good at asking questions are enormous. Which of the following questions would you find the *easiest* to answer?—or the *most difficult* to answer?

- Have you listened to any classical music on the radio or your stereo this past week?
- Which type of music do you listen to most?
- How do you decide what type of music you will allow your children to purchase?

The first is a *simple* question. It can be easily answered with a yes or no. It doesn't give you much valuable information, but it's a great way to begin a conversation, knowing that you aren't going to make the other person uncomfortable. You want it to be a question pertaining to your area of expertise, so you patiently watch and listen for an opening. To get there, you can ask simple questions about the other person's family and work and anything else that will encourage him or her to do what most people like best— talk about themselves.

The second question is *factual*. It begins with words like *what, who, which,* and *when.* The factual answers others give will point to their preferences. The answers begin to provide information that's more helpful. But there is still some vital information that you do not know.

The third question is *complex*. The answers will give you factual information plus a whole lot more. You will learn how the person thinks and what he or she believes is important. That's the type of information that points to areas of dissatisfaction. This type of question often begins with *how* or *what steps you take to do something.* However, avoid asking *why.* That question puts people on the spot, and affluent prospects will not appreciate being in that position.

When asking questions, begin simple. Ask for a few facts, and then you can start digging deeper. You do that by continually circling through simple, factual, and complex questions. When you sense where there might be an area of dissatisfaction, you can simply ask: "Are you satisfied with X (product, service, brand, salesperson, or solution)?"—or—"What would you like to see improved about X the next time?"—or—"What steps do you plan to take the next time you search for X?"

When do you make your "sales pitch"? The fact is, you began the moment you started asking questions that gradually drew the person like a magnet to what you offer. When you sense that prospects are ready to sit down and get serious about changing their situation, you can suggest doing precisely that. You invite them into the carefully orchestrated affluent sales environment you learned to create in Chapter 3. When you meet with them again, you continue probing. Along the way, you watch and listen carefully for any buying signals.

DETECTING BUYING SIGNALS

When you are asking simple, factual, and complex questions in order to identify areas of dissatisfaction or to determine whether prospects are ready to make a buying decision, you will also be explaining what you offer and answering their questions. At some point, you must ask if they are ready to buy. But how will you know if and when they are ready? They will let you know, if you watch and listen for those buying signals. Here's what you will see and hear:

- They nod in agreement and give positive responses.
- They lean their body forward, and their tone of voice becomes relaxed.
- They express a strong preference when you present alternative solutions and then ask them which solution they prefer.
- Their questions switch to things such as cost, when can you start, or how long they will have to wait.
- They make a strong verbal commitment, such as "Sounds good," to the things you say.
- They make a negative/positive statement such as, "Of course, I wouldn't be able to take delivery until we get back from Europe."
- They reach for your promotional materials, ask to look at them, and begin making positive comments or asking questions about specific items.
- They ask for assurance with questions like, "That's interesting. Which do you think would be best?"
- They comment on how good it will feel to have someone like you serving them.

It takes only a couple of these signals to clearly indicate that you need to close the sale.

CLOSING THE SALE

Do not hesitate to try to close the sale. Studies continually show that the vast majority of people who sell do not close the sale for one simple reason: They don't ask. Some studies say that 50 percent fail to ask; others suggest it's as high as 62 percent. But that's not all. Another 35 percent will ask for the order, accept whatever excuse is given for not buying at that time, and then never ask again. You now know *when* to ask, but *what* to ask is equally as important.

There are three things to which your affluent prospects must agree, and all three must be "closed" before you can conclude that you have made the sale:

1. *Acceptance of the solution you believe they prefer.* That includes the full package: products, configurations, services, and support.
2. *Acceptance of the selling price and all associated costs.* Full cost disclosure is vital.
3. *Their decision to buy now.* Never assume that because the first two are acceptable, the third is a foregone conclusion.

The following closing technique enables you to progress through the three levels, confirming each before going on to the next. If prospects resist, this technique will enable you to know exactly where the problem lies. We call it *the solution close:*

1. *Content:* We have talked at length about [describe *what* they will be buying]. From our discussion, I believe we can help you [describe the *solution* it will give them]. We can have everything delivered and set up for you by [give a promised delivery and set up by date]. Does this accurately describe what you are expecting?
2. *Cost:* The total cost will be [give the total cost]. That includes [give a cost breakdown]. Payment is due [explain]. Is that your understanding as well?
3. *Commitment:* I have the sales order right here. Would you please sign here?

You may have to draw up a contract or some other type of agreement, but you should have prospects sign something at that moment so that they make both a mental and physical commitment to the sale.

At any of those three decision points, they may resist your close. It could come in any of the following forms:

- That's not exactly what I had in mind.
- I'd like to check with a couple of other companies first.
- That's more than I had intended to pay.
- I want to think about it for a while.

If this resistance or something like it occurs, you can now relate it back to the level you just completed, making it much easier to overcome their objections. If the content is involved, you can make adjustments before moving on to the cost. Otherwise, their objection to the cost may relate back to the content. If you have closed successfully on both content and cost before receiving this type of response, you will know it is more of a stall than an objection. If they are stalling, there's a problem that you probably aren't even aware of, and you won't find out what it is unless you ask. Here are some questions you can use:

- Are there some other issues that need to be resolved first?
- Would you mind telling me what's wrong with what I've suggested?
- Have I offended you in any way with what I've proposed?

Remember that you are using these questions to try to begin a dialog that will take you to the heart of the issue. If something is truly wrong, you cannot advance the sale until it is resolved.

There is one final aspect of becoming magnetic that could be created as a result of everything you have done to this point. All you have to do is reach out and grab it. Think back through the process you have used to find affluent prospects—discovering what they want, shaping a solution that best meets their needs, watching and listening for buying signals, and then closing the sale. What type of relationship has that process enabled you to form with your new customer or client?

It's all about creating face-time and developing a professional relationship with some real depth to it. This is the type of win-win relationship that enables you to ask them for introductions and referrals with high expectations. There's no stopping you now.

SUMMARY

Your prospects need to feel a gentle and irresistible tug, beckoning them toward what you can offer them. Your efforts to attract affluent prospects to you must be a high priority and a planned activity.

Instead of depending on mass mailings, national advertising campaigns, or simply cold calling, you need to concentrate on the power of networking and word-of-mouth influence to achieve your prospecting goals. You also do not want to come across as a salesperson, so simply telling anyone who will listen about your great products and services is the worst thing you can do.

You need qualified prospects—those who are *dissatisfied* because they have unfulfilled goals and aspirations, they want to be the first to try something, they have a problem they want solved, they have an opportunity they want to pursue, they have products or services that are not meeting their needs, or a supplier they once trusted is not meeting their needs or standards.

Introductions and referrals are the two most effective ways to attract affluent prospects because these methods accelerate the trust-building process. When mixing and socializing, the questions you ask will open doors quickly. Learn to initially ask simple, then factual, and, finally, more complex questions. When asking questions and responding to your affluent prospects' questions, you will begin to observe and hear buying signals that let you know they are ready to be sold.

Closing the sale is best done as a three-step process. Make certain prospects accept the solution you believe they prefer. Then make certain they accept the selling price and all associated costs. Finally,

Research Facts

➤ Our research shows that affluent people typically do not look to salespeople to find what they need. They depend on friends, family, colleagues, and acquaintances whose opinions they trust.

➤ Affluent buyers conduct extensive research before making a purchase, and that research is increasingly done on the Internet.

➤ Postpurchase service ranked as a "very important" piece of criteria for ensuring repeat business, which is essential for stimulating word-of-mouth influence.

confirm their decision to buy now. If they resist your close, ask additional questions to determine what could be blocking the sale.

TAKING ACTION

- Set up your *prospecting plan*. Identify the current affluent customers or clients and other affluent individuals you can contact to ask for introductions and referrals. Commit to a set number of contacts at the beginning of the week, and then measure your progress at the end of the week.
- Review the six types of dissatisfaction that your affluent prospects might be experiencing. Then complete a *product and service profile* indicating the features, advantages, solutions, and evidence you can provide for each product and service you offer.
- Practice your Introductions and referral scripts.
- Practice the kinds of questions you will use when mixing and socializing.
- Memorize the list of buying signals so you will recognize them instinctively.
- Practice closing the sale so you do not overlook any of the three areas you need to close.

- Practice the questions you will use when an affluent prospect resists your close.
- Create your process for taking the lead in postpurchase service.
- Determine which existing clients need to be contacted about postpurchase service.
- Begin your prospecting efforts, focusing on your fixed daily activities.
- Initiate an activity designed to strengthen your reputation.

8

BECOMING EVEN MORE MAGNETIC: INTERNET SAVVY

Remember from Chapter 7 the magnet that Joan Popek's mother claimed was buried in the middle of Roswell, New Mexico? It has now been dug up and relocated somewhere out in cyberspace where it is creating a pull that the affluent find impossible to resist.

In only 10 short years, the number of Internet users has grown from around 16 million to over 716 million worldwide, including about 62 percent of the U.S. population. The fastest growing online income group earns between $100,000 and $150,000 a year. In fact, a recent study by washingtonpost.com and Nielsen/Net Ratings shows that affluent adults rely heavily on the Internet to both research and make purchases. They also found that affluent adults access the Web nearly every day, using it far more than any other media. Here are the important facts from that research:

- Daytime (8 A.M. to 5 P.M.) is the best time to reach the affluent. They have professional and managerial positions that give them more freedom to access the Internet. The at-work Internet audience is about 50 million, and 86 percent have broadband access. Consequently, 60 percent of e-commerce sales come from people at work.
- The Internet is the dominant media vehicle for reaching the affluent during the day—about five times more effective

than television and equally as influential as newspapers. Of those surveyed, 58 percent had been influenced by a newspaper ad to make a purchase in the past six months, and 55 percent were influenced by an online ad.

- Virtually all affluent adult shoppers use the Internet to research or make buying decisions. Over 90 percent surveyed said they have used the Internet for automobile, computer, or travel purchases.

Our 2004 APD Research left no doubt that the affluent give highest credibility to the opinions of family members and trusted friends when deciding where to look for major purchase options. When making the purchase decision, however, those opinions carry much less weight. The criteria that move to the top confirm what other research has shown. In order of priority, the five items that respondents said were *very important* to them when making their final choice were as follows:

1. Finding the right set of features.
2. Finding the best possible option through careful evaluation and comparison.
3. Finding a discounted or sale price.
4. Responsiveness of sales and service people.
5. What reviews, testimonials, and other sources say about product and service quality.

They look to the evidence that they uncover themselves, and then they consider the review and testimonials of others. Have no doubt that affluent buyers are confident in their decision-making ability. In Chapter 2, we listed seven factors that typically drive the major purchase discussions of the affluent. The fourth factor bears repeating here:

4. They will do the research and trust their own judgment to define value in their own terms. Then they will go wherever

that quest for value takes them, even if it is a web site or a warehouse club.

The preceding research data should be no surprise. Daytime broadband access, the ability to visit 36 million web sites from their office, the quest for value, and the desire to do the research themselves all work together to create an irresistible magnet that daily pulls the affluent consumer into cyberspace. The message is clear—you better be there to greet them. In this chapter, we show you how.

CONTINUE WHAT YOU ARE DOING, PLUS MORE

In Chapter 7, your efforts to attract affluent prospects took the form of introductions, referrals, mixing, and socializing. You do *not* want to replace those activities, but you *do* want to capitalize on the Internet's potential for expanding and enriching your efforts. To do that, you need to diligently implement the following steps:

1. Make certain that you *obtain the e-mail address* of each customer/client and prospect, along with his or her name and other important information. Greeting the affluent online does not mean having your photo appear on your company's web site, though you may want to eventually do that as well. E-mail is the most frequently used part of the Internet, and it has now become the preferred business communication tool. Do not let all those articles about spam and security fool you. If you follow the recent CAN-SPAM legislation guidelines, e-mail will provide you with the fastest and most effective way to communicate with people. People tend to read e-mail sooner and more often than they check voice mail. E-mail enables you to include live links to web pages and include document, graphical, audio, and even short video attachments. With the right software or online service, you can send the same e-mail message to all your prospects or to a select group automatically. You can even create several sequential messages and

automatically schedule them to go out on prescribed dates. Here are the tools you need:

- A computerized contact management database for storing each prospect's name, e-mail address, and other valuable information.
- A strong e-mail program (called e-mail client software) that will enable you to send, receive, store, and effectively manage your e-mail messages.

Some programs, such as Microsoft Outlook, can effectively serve both purposes.

2. Find out the *actual search terms* (called "keywords" and "keyphrases") people on the Internet use to find what you offer. You can identify the following:

- The exact keywords and keyphrases people are using to search for the information, ideas, solutions, products, and services you offer.
- The average number of times each keyword or phrase has been used each day over the past 30 days.

We have set up a *Free KEYWORD Suggestion Tool* on a special web page for this purpose. Go to www.oechsli.com/keywords. This web page provides complete instructions, including how to organize and use the keywords and phrases that are created by the tool. Remember that there are 36 million web sites out there, but only a very small percentage offer what you offer. Internet users go to search engines such as Google to find those web sites. They enter the keywords and phrases they have in mind, and the search engine lists web sites that are relevant to the words and phrases they entered. That's where the KEYWORD Suggestion Tool obtains those words and phrases. People usually limit their visits to web sites listed on the first page of the search engine. The more diligent will go to the second and third pages. People will typically visit up to 10 web sites, so that should be your next step.

3. Use your list of keywords and keyphrases to *explore the web sites people select to visit* so you can see what they see when they go there. Then you can use that information to *determine how your competitor's offerings are positioned and priced.* Here's what you need to do:

- Go to www.google.com. Google is currently the largest and most used search engine.
- From your list, identify the top 10 or so keywords or phrases that you feel people would most likely use to find what you offer.
- Type one of those keywords or phrases in the "Search the Web" box at the top. Place quotation marks around that keyword or phrase. Google will pull up the web sites that use that exact word or phrase.
- Start visiting web sites. Either start at the top of the first page and work down, or begin with the web site that you believe people using that keyword or phrase would most likely select. When you visit that web site, begin to make notes about the information, ideas, and solutions they offer—and how they have positioned and priced their products and services. Repeat that same process for other web sites you believe they would select. When you visit a web site that is so cluttered and confusing that you can't really figure out who and what they are, simply click the back button on your browser and return to the Google page. That's probably what your prospects and customers/clients will do. However, don't click back simply because you are becoming impatient. Take at least 30 seconds to explore that web page. Studies show that people typically leave a web site after

about 10 seconds if they cannot answer that "Am I in the right place?" question satisfactorily; so 30 seconds should be adequate for your purposes.

Once you have completed the previous steps, you can use your notes to determine how to position what you offer in the e-mail messages that you send. As you explore competitor web sites, look for three things:

1. Areas where those web sites are strong—and what you can do to match and compete with them
2. Areas where they are weak—and what you can do to demonstrate your advantages
3. Areas that are missing—and, again, what you can do to demonstrate your advantages

As you work to complete this exercise, you will be amazed at all the creative ways you will find to communicate the benefits and competitive advantages of what you offer. When you begin sending e-mails, do not make competitive comparisons in your message. But do make certain that you emphasize the right things so that when your prospects and customers or clients are doing their research, what you offer becomes their benchmark of comparison. As you learned in Chapter 2, that's the way the affluent prefer to shop.

4. Launch a consistent, compelling, and creative *e-mail marketing campaign* using any or all of the following:

- Before you send out any e-mail to prospects, customers, or clients, create a signature file that will appear at the end of each e-mail you send. Your signature file should contain the following information: Your name, your organization, contact information (phone and fax numbers), your URL (web site address) and e-mail address, and a brief "tag line" that explains some benefit of doing business with you. You can change your tag line as appropriate. Check your e-mail program for instructions on how to set up a signature file.

- Right after your first encounter, send a *brief* e-mail saying how great it was to get to know him or her. Include a review of anything substantive you discussed and a confirmation of any future appointments you made.
- Before every appointment, send a brief e-mail confirming when and where you are meeting plus the purpose for that meeting. After the appointment, send another brief e-mail with basically the same approach used following your first encounter.
- Schedule special events before and after normal business hours, and send e-mail invitations to customers/clients and select prospects. Include the specific reasons you believe they will benefit from being there.
- Use e-mail to announce new products or services, closeout sales, and other specials. Schedule a special time for customers/clients and prospects to shop before or after normal business hours and a day or two before the products or services are available to the general public.
- Create an e-mail newsletter, making certain that you provide useful information and minimize the sales pitch. Rather than sending it automatically to your list, consider asking contacts to "subscribe." This is called "opt-in," and it is an important part of complying with the CAN-SPAM legislation.

The most important part of any e-mail message is the subject line. People look there first to decide whether to read or delete the message. Beyond that, make your messages personal, conversational, and brief. If you have a web site, you can highlight specific products and/or services at the end of your message with live links to the web site pages where they can learn more (and buy).

CREATE A COMPELLING ONLINE PRESENCE

If you do not have your own web site, you should consider launching one soon, even if you service a small regional or local market. There's an important reason for this.

Go to www.google.com. When you arrive, notice the links at the top: Web Images, Groups, News, Froogle, and more. Click on "more . . ." Then click on "Google Local." This is a recently added service, and other major search engines are doing the same. Start entering keywords and phrases from your list, and then enter your location in the "US address, city & state, or zip" box. Do you have a web site listed there? If not, you should—and you must, no later than 2005. Why the deadline, you might ask? Since the affluent use the Internet extensively for research, they will soon discover that Google and the other major search engines have added local area search capabilities.

Whether you have a web site or are just now becoming convinced you should, I have great news for you. You are already doing what most businesses fail to do. Finding and collecting the keywords and phrases your prospects and customers or clients use to find what you offer has application far beyond your e-mail marketing campaign. There are four other benefits you will gain by taking the time and making the effort to create that keyword and phrase list and explore competitive web sites:

1. You will use those keywords and phrases to *define your unique Internet niche*—and to *describe your business* to others. This is often called a "value statement" or "business proposition." When using this description on your web site, on every document and article you create, and in your conversations, you will do so knowing that you are talking the language of the people you want to attract. Talk about becoming a magnet!

2. You will also use those keywords and phrases to *describe what you offer:*

- In the information, instructions, ideas, and solutions you will use on your web site to demonstrate your value and "pull" targeted web site visitors to the point of sale.
- In describing the features, advantages, solutions, and evidence of the products and services you offer on your web site.
- In describing the items you offer free on your web site in exchange for the person's name and e-mail address. That could include a newsletter, an e-mail course, special reports, e-books, or whatever type of document is appropriate for your business. This is another way to keep building your prospect database and at the same time provide something of value to the prospect.

3. You will use those keywords and phrases *on your web site* to:
   - Create your logo and write a tag line that will convince targeted visitors within five seconds that they are in the right place.
   - Help you decide how to organize your web site so that targeted visitors can easily determine where they want to go next.
   - Create titles, headings, and content that relate to the interests and needs of targeted visitors.

4. You will use those keywords and phrases in your *promotional strategy* to:
   - Optimize your web site pages so that search engines will view those pages as relevant to the keywords and phrases you use when you submit those web pages to be listed. That's what it takes to be included within the first 10 to 20 listings.
   - Guide every other online and offline promotional strategy and method you use.

Many of the 36 million web sites are resting peacefully in the Internet graveyard. They are nothing more than online billboards, brochures, or catalogs that simply list products; and they are rarely visited. Your web site needs to be much more than that.

The purpose of having a web site is to "pull" targeted visitors to the point of sale. To do that, you first have to attract the right visitors to your web site. Effective search engine listings and e-mail marketing campaigns will enable you to accomplish that goal. How your web site is designed will determine whether targeted visitors stay long enough to explore further and take advantage of the effective way you have positioned and priced your products and services.

Everything—absolutely everything—begins with selecting the right keywords and phrases. You now know how to do that. Many people attempting to launch an Internet business do not.

MEET THE EXPECTATIONS OF
AFFLUENT WEB SITE VISITORS

In a recent study of affluent investors, Forrester Research (March 31, 2004) discovered that those investors who work with a financial advisor are more active online with their investments than those investors who go it alone. Despite that, investment firms are continually criticized for neglecting their web sites. The study's Executive Summary puts it this way: "These stale, ill-conceived sites undermine the relationships between clients and their advisors and need to be fixed." The study points out that this issue extends to every luxury e-tailer trying to appeal to affluent online shoppers. Note carefully what the research uncovered:

- The most common mistake is assuming that affluent shoppers want to be dazzled by fancy, entertaining web sites. Many build web sites loaded with graphics such as Flash that load slowly and require additional browser plug-ins to work properly. What the affluent want is a unique shopping experience, not a dazzling experience.
- Most of all, affluent shoppers want control over their shopping experience, easy access to quality customer service, and guaranteed protection of their personal information.

Here are several tips for correcting those problems:

- People go to the Internet for information, not entertainment. The most important element on each web page is the text. Design elements and graphics should be used to create the right image and support the text.
- Make it easy for web site visitors to find the information they want. That's how your web site becomes personalized for each visitor. Provide as much information as you can about each product and service with links to other information and helpful resources. Include a smart search engine so visitors can find information from anywhere on your web site. By allowing visitors to create their own pathway through your web site, it becomes their web site—and they're hooked!
- Clearly communicate product and service costs—the total costs—before they click on the "buy" button. Don't force them to wait until they have first provided you with personal information.
- Make shopping simple, with as few steps as possible. Also simplify the return process.
- Provide quality customer service.
- Post a privacy policy on your web site, and follow that policy to the letter. Protect any information a visitor or customer/client gives you.

Having a web site that undermines your relationship with your customers/clients and prospects makes absolutely no sense. Remember that three questions are continually going through each web site visitor's mind: Am I in the right place? Where should I go next? Can I trust these people? When you decide to launch your own web site, have everyone who helps you read this chapter. Discuss it with them, and make certain that they understand and will help you implement each point. Continually ask, "How are you going to . . . ?" type questions to confirm that they are on the same page as you.

One final comment about searching for keywords and phrases and visiting related competitive web sites. That exercise was suggested for the specific reasons noted, but you will quickly discover it has benefits far beyond that. You can take the preceding principles and tips and use them to evaluate every web site you visit. It won't be long before you are able to clearly differentiate among the good, the bad, and the ugly. As you look at an aspect of web site design that does or does not impress you, enter that aspect as a keyword or phrase in your favorite search engine. Up will come a list of web sites that will enable you to quickly expand your understanding of that area.

The great thing about the Internet is that you can use it to expand your expertise in an area so quickly that it makes your head spin. In this day and age, the more you understand about Internet marketing, the better.

SUMMARY

Daytime broadband access, access to 36 million web sites, the quest for value, and the desire to do their own research is pulling the affluent to the Internet during daytime office hours. Affluent Americans are the fastest growing group of Internet users. You better be there to greet them.

You need to capitalize on the Internet's potential for expanding and enriching your prospecting efforts. You also need to have your own web site if you hope to create a compelling online presence.

The affluent do not want to be dazzled by fancy, entertaining web sites. The affluent go to the Internet for information, not entertainment. Most of all, they want control over their shopping experience, easy access to quality customer service, and guaranteed protection of their personal information.

When people visit your web site, they must find the answers to three questions within about 20 seconds: Am I in the right place? Where should I go next? Can I trust these people?

Research Facts

➤ In only 10 years, the Internet has grown from 16 million to over 716 million users worldwide—which includes about 62 percent of the U.S. population.

➤ The fastest growing online income user group is those earning between $100,000 and $150,000 a year.

➤ The best time to reach the affluent is from 8 A.M. to 5 P.M. Sixty percent of e-commerce comes from people at work.

➤ Virtually all affluent adult shoppers use the Internet as their primary research tool for assistance in making major purchase decisions.

➤ The 2004 APD Research respondents said that they research major purchase decisions and the Internet is their primary research vehicle.

TAKING ACTION

• Set up a computerized database. Begin gathering and entering the e-mail address and name of each customer or client and prospect along with other important information. Enter the data daily so you can begin using that database.

• After you determine the actual search terms people use to find what you offer on the Internet, begin exploring the web sites visited by people using those terms. Use that information to determine how your competitors' offerings are positioned and priced.

• Launch a consistent, compelling, and creative e-mail marketing campaign.

• Create your own web site. Place the address of that web site on your calling cards and every other printed document you use.

9

MASTERING RITZ-CARLTON SERVICE AND FEDEX EFFICIENCY

Whether or not you provide quality service has a significant influence on affluent major purchase decision making.

—FACTOID, 2004 APD RESEARCH

While staying at the Ritz-Carlton in Phoenix a few years ago, I happened to overhear a guest having an intense conversation with a Ritz-Carlton employee in the concierge lounge. It was the nastiness of this guest that caught my attention. The guy was waving a small card in a mocking gesture and grilling the poor Ritz-Carlton employee with obnoxious questions like, "So what gives you the right to have a credo saying you are ladies and gentlemen serving ladies and gentlemen? Is that why I have to pay $250 a night?"

Talk about grace under pressure! The training that the Ritz-Carlton employee had received served him well, and it was evident that he was a true believer in everything his company represented. I was astonished as I watched him patiently explain every aspect of the Ritz-Carlton credo that was published on the little card being waved in his face by the insulting guest. Curious about the actual content of that card, I asked another Ritz-Carlton employee if I could take a peek at it. She promptly placed one in my hand and told me to keep it. I'm not sure why, but I have kept that card in my wallet ever since. By the way, I discovered later that the obnoxious guest grilling the Ritz-Carlton employee was a well-known comedian who was working on material for his upcoming show.

Ritz-Carlton has become the standard that many use for measuring the quality of the service they receive elsewhere. Catering to the affluent since its incorporation in 1983, Ritz-Carlton has received all the major awards that the hospitality industry can bestow. They are also the only hotel to win the Malcom Baldrige National Quality Award and the first and only service company to win the award twice, in 1992 and 1999. They dedicate over 100 hours of total quality management training to every employee—which is possibly why our comedian friend chose the Ritz-Carlton credo as the object of his humor.

FedEx has created a similar standard for operational efficiency. Many affluent consumers use other overnight carriers, whether it's the Postal Service, UPS, Express Airborne, or DHL. All of these companies have invested millions of dollars trying to convince the public that they are just as dependable as, and less expensive than, FedEx. But in my office, if something absolutely, positively has to get to its destination at a prescribed time, we use FedEx.

Whether it's fair or not, Ritz-Carlton service and FedEx efficiency have become the standards on which the affluent will measure you and your organization. Other organizations are their equal, but possibly with the inclusion of Lexus dealerships, these well-known service organizations have emerged as the benchmark that the affluent use. If someone in your organization appears a bit rushed, is distracted, or becomes slightly annoyed, dissatisfaction will begin to creep into the customer's mind. That is not how the people at the Ritz-Carlton treat their clients, and it should not happen in your organization.

In Chapter 7, we focused on three criteria that our 2004 APD Research said had the greatest influence on whether an affluent buyer would use the same product or service provider again for a major purchase. There were actually seven criteria that at least 40 percent of the respondents identified as having considerable influence over that decision. We list them here along with the percent of respondents who placed each item in the *considerable influence* category. Take special notice of where "lowest price" appears in this list. The seven criteria are:

1. Any problems I encountered were resolved quickly and satisfactorily—90.3 percent.
2. They provided good service following my purchase—81.8 percent.
3. They provided the information I needed to make a satisfactory purchase decision—69.5 percent.
4. Their guarantees of satisfaction were clearly defined—65.8 percent.
5. The brand I prefer is available through them—63.0 percent.
6. The people who represented them were friendly and helpful—62.5 percent.
7. They offered the lowest price available—44.3 percent.

Coincidently, I happen to know two individuals who purchased the same 50-inch plasma entertainment system with all the bells and whistles. One is my brother, and the other is one of my regular tennis partners. Since my brother lives in Connecticut and my tennis partner lives in North Carolina, these purchases were made totally independent of each other.

Both went to a friend they respected who recommended the system they eventually purchased. Both conducted research using the Internet to study the various features, options, competitive products, consumer reviews, price points, and purchasing options. At the point of purchase, their paths veered off into different directions. My brother followed the initial advice of his friend and purchased the entire system, including installation, from the web site his friend had recommended. After selecting the system based on his Internet research, my tennis partner shopped around the local electronic stores and bought from the store where the salesperson seemed knowledgeable and assured him that they could install, service, and troubleshoot the system.

Both have had their 50-inch plasma entertainment system for approximately nine months and thoroughly enjoy it. However, neither would recommend their system when I asked. That seemed a bit curious to me, so I asked why. Here is what they told me.

Both my brother and my friend had considerable hassles getting the initial installation completed to the point that it was "idiot proof" enough for them to understand how the system worked. In each case, the installers overlooked "little things" that continually delayed their ability to use the system. Both continue to have minor follow-up issues, and that's what causes them to pause when anyone asks, "Where would you suggest I go to get a system like that?" Why? Because the problems they encountered were not resolved quickly and satisfactorily. Both the Internet company and the local electronic store used contract installers, and the service each provided was lousy. Neither came close to Ritz-Carlton-level service supported by FedEx efficiency, the only standards acceptable to the affluent.

I recognize that you may not be in control of your company's corporate quality and service policy making, because if you work for a large firm, they set the policies, handle fulfillment, and service all warranty work. But the truth is, too many companies cut corners in these areas. The marketing department makes all the seductive before-purchase promises, but you, my fellow sales friend, are left to deliver what was promised. Therefore, I encourage you to pay attention to the preceding list, which tells you exactly what needs to be done to please your affluent clients and customers.

ACCEPT PERSONAL RESPONSIBILITY

Your affluent customers or clients recognize that not everything is within your control, but they do expect you to have a strong working knowledge of your company's quality and service process. They also expect you to take the initiative to compensate for any deficiencies. You must know what your company does well, what they are working hard to improve, and where potential problems exist. You must then become proactive in your efforts to lessen the impact of all those factors on your customers or clients.

Remember Bob and Mary in Chapter 1 and their car purchases? Imagine the positive word-of-mouth Bob could have generated if the original salesperson who assisted his wife in purchasing her convertible sports car had provided her with his personal cell phone number and urged her to call him first if she ever encountered any problems with her car. That salesperson could not guarantee that the special order tires would be kept in stock, but he could have stepped in and made certain that the inconvenience did not burden Mary in any way. Unfortunately, the salesperson fell into the trap of assuming that service is someone else's responsibility. If I were a betting man, I would wager that this salesperson is not on the path to becoming affluent—at least not as a salesperson.

Following is a simple checklist that identifies areas within your control that can assist you in elevating your ability to provide Ritz-Carlton service and FedEx efficiency to affluent customers or clients:

Service and Efficiency Checklist

- Learn your company's service policies and procedures, and evaluate how well your local service department adheres to them. Check things such as warranty work, turnaround time, the hours they are open for business, and anything else that is important to getting through the service maze.
- Build a personal relationship with every individual in your service areas and especially your service manager. Establish a good telephone relationship with any long-distance service personnel who might be involved with your customers or clients. This might prove difficult if your firm is outsourcing customer support overseas, but when there is a will, there is a way.
- Recognize your company's service limitations, and then be clear with your customers or clients about how you will personally work with them to fill in those gaps. They want to know what you will do, not what you cannot do.

- Follow up periodically with every customer or client to determine whether anything is not working and how you can be of assistance.
- Stay current on things such as special offers, rebates, discounts, and recalls—and contact each customer or client prior to any formal announcement.
- Provide a personal phone number (cell phone, pager) so customers or clients can contact you immediately if they encounter any problems or have any questions.

Providing Ritz-Carlton service with FedEx efficiency is not rocket science. Mostly, it's a personal mind-set. You either commit yourself to excellence, or you do not. You either constantly look for ways to improve your service, or you do not. This personal commitment has nothing to do with corporate policies and procedures, and it will never guarantee your customers or clients will be totally free from problems. What it will do is convince your customers or clients that you are there for them and that they can feel totally free to contact you for anything, anytime.

DO YOUR HOMEWORK

In Chapter 8, we showed you how to research your competitors using the Internet. I now ask you to do that again, but this time to determine the quality of your competitors' service. You will have to go beyond the promises they make on their web sites and in their television advertising campaigns, promotional literature, or any other form of marketing communication. The key is to experience exactly what your competitors' affluent prospects and customers or clients experience. Your goal is to evaluate the quality of that experience and look for ways that you can create a competitive service and efficiency advantage.

This is an exercise we periodically use at the Oechsli Institute, and every time we learn something that helps us improve. Just like you, we are always striving to raise the bar. I am continually amazed at how frequently our detective work (we use secret shoppers) creates surprises. Often it's a well-known consultant or firm that fails to live up to their marketing promises. At first I was shocked, but I now find it to be empowering.

Whether you are selling a service or a product, the basic tenets of this detective work are the same. You want to know everything possible about your competition from an affluent prospect's perspective—the quality of their product or service, their availability, any technical differences, their level of personal service, follow-through, and so on. You want to assess both strengths and weaknesses. Here is a checklist that can assist you in getting started:

- Create a separate file folder for each competitor.
- Have someone other than you (a secret shopper) contact each competitor, expressing interest in their products or services.
- Create a script for each secret shopper to follow that includes questions about quality, service, availability, price, and warranty. Make certain that your secret shopper takes accurate notes.
- If possible, have your secret shopper ask for information to be mailed. You want to determine competitors' responsiveness and collect all possible collateral materials.
- Have your secret shoppers complete a form that includes a checklist to use in evaluating basic service issues, such as whether competitors were pleasant, accommodating, responsive, knowledgeable, and professional.
- Whenever possible, determine the "position" that your competitor holds in the mind of your affluent market.

You can add or subtract from this list as you see fit. The idea is to determine which of your competitors is best-in-class and why. From this platform of intelligence gathering, you will be able to create a personal benchmark that is tailored specifically to your business. As you complete each competitor evaluation, ask yourself: "Have I discovered anything new that will help me achieve a higher level of Ritz-Carlton service, backed by FedEx efficiency?" If your answer is yes, do something about it. According to our 2004 APD Research, evaluating and comparing options have a significant impact in the final major purchase decision. If you perform the role of a trusted source of information, someone who can assist an affluent prospect in his or her prepurchase research, you will have a distinct advantage.

CREATE YOUR VALUE PROPOSITION AND ELEVATOR SPEECH

A credo is not simply a statement; it's a *system of belief.* President Harry Truman had a sign on his desk that read, "The Buck Stops Here." He became known not simply for the statement, but for his efforts to live up to it. The statement became a brief, simple expression of what others could expect of him.

Your challenge is to quantify, communicate, and demonstrate your value to every affluent prospect and customer or client whenever needed and at any given time. Once you have the various elements of that value clear in your mind, it would be great if you could find a way to let prospects and customers or clients know what they can expect from you. Rather than *credo,* we prefer the term *Value Proposition. Value* shifts the focus, challenging you to think about how useful and important your products and services are to your customers or clients. *Proposition* is "a plan suggested for acceptance," reminding you that whatever value you believe you offer, it must be accepted by those to whom it is offered.

The object of a Value Proposition is to create a conceptual framework from which every aspect of your professional relationship can unfold. Since it's impossible to highlight every detail of a future relationship, you need to create a word picture that is crystal clear and free of ambiguity so that it quickly and simply communicates the benefits of doing business with you. An example of how simple this can be from an article titled "Doctors' New

Practices Offer Deluxe Service for Deluxe Fee" appeared on the front page of the January 15, 2002, *New York Times:*

> Patients who pay will get amenities and attention that virtually no managed care practice can provide nowadays: round-the-clock cell phone access to doctors, same-day appointments, nutrition and exercise physiology exams at patients homes or health clubs, and doctors to accompany them to specialists.

The deluxe fee these patients are paying is $4,000 a year, and that's on top of the medical costs covered by their health insurance. If the affluent people they have targeted value those amenities and that attention, they will pay. Using the information provided in this article, these two doctors could craft a simple Value Proposition that would go something like this:

> An exclusive medical practice where all of our patients have 24/7 cell phone access to doctors, receive same-day appointments, receive in-home nutrition and exercise counseling, and have one of our doctors coordinate and accompany them to special medical procedures.

This could get boiled down even further to:

> Exclusive medical practice providing 24/7 cell phone access, same-day appointments, nutrition and exercise counseling, and personal coordination of all medical procedures.

Value Propositions could also be created for three of the affluent sales environment descriptions in Chapter 3.

1. The office furniture retailer in California who specializes in selling an upscale home office concept: *Upscale home office environments that are creatively designed, space efficient, expertly installed, and fully coordinated to match your taste and décor.*
2. The photography studio that targets the affluent using a concept they call "life-cycle selling": *A unique life-cycle*

photography plan that ensures we will be there to capture your special moments in time each time they occur, with photographs that blend inward qualities with outward appearance and are taken in settings that tastefully express your lifestyle.

3. The window coverings dealer who focuses on selling to homeowners using the concept of a beautiful room: *Exclusive window coverings made of the highest quality materials, carefully coordinated to beautify your room, expertly installed, and fully guaranteed.*

The next step is to reduce your Value Proposition statement to a single, thought-provoking statement. I often refer to this as an *elevator speech,* meaning it is brief and stimulating enough to catch someone's attention if they hear all of it in the duration of a short elevator ride. I got the idea of creating elevator speeches years ago at a black-tie affair in Washington, DC, hosted by my friend and colleague Somers White. Present was a collection of consultants, motivational speakers, lawyers, and politicians—all salespeople in one form or another. Right before being served our main course, Somers grabbed a microphone, delivered a welcoming introduction, and proceeded to walk around the room asking a handful of people to stand up and deliver an elevator speech that would explain to the group what they did for a living without using typical labels (lawyer, consultant, etc.) and to do it in the time it would take to travel by elevator from the 10th floor to the lobby.

The objective was to be descriptive, informative, and entertaining. Although each individual performing this exercise had been briefed well in advance, most appeared tongue-tied. It was tough to succinctly describe your professional identity in that brief amount of time.

For me, the light bulb went on. From that point forward, although I still help people develop Value Proposition statements, I emphasize brevity. Drawing once again on the affluent sales environment examples from Chapter 3, here are possible elevator speeches for each:

- The office furniture retailer: *We design and install space-efficient home office environments.*
- The photographer: *We specialize in lifestyle photography that captures your special moments each time they occur.*
- The window coverings dealer: *We transform windows to enhance the beauty of your room.*

When you deliver your elevator speech, your greatest hope is that it will create interest and make the person who heard or read it curious enough to ask you for more information. Following is a series of questions designed to help you craft your Value Proposition and ultimately your elevator speech:

- How would you describe the *profile* of your "ideal" customer or client?

  _____

  _____

  _____

  _____

- What do you want to *characterize the relationship* you have with your "ideal" customer or client?

  _____

  _____

  _____

  _____

- What do your current customers or clients *value most* about the products, services, and solutions you offer?

  _____

  _____

  _____

  _____

- What do your customers or clients *value that you do not presently offer?*

  _____

  _____

  _____

  _____

- Based on your answers to the preceding questions, what *value-enhancement changes* do you need to make?

  _____

  _____

  _____

  _____

- If a customer or client were talking about you to a family member, friend, or colleague, how would you want him or her to *describe the value* you provide?

  _____

  _____

  _____

  _____

The purpose of the exercise is to force you to think. These questions are not easy to answer, which is why we don't ask them as often as we should. Add other questions if you like.

Your Value Proposition and briefer elevator speech must communicate the real value that you bring to each of your customers or clients by consistently performing beyond their expectations. A good Value Proposition statement/elevator speech will help you gain mind share. It should also compel you to continually work at becoming better at what you do.

After thoughtfully answering each of the preceding questions, you should be ready to draft your Value Proposition. Once that is complete, you can condense that proposition into your elevator speech. So let's give it a try. Write Version 1—review your answers to the questions once again—evaluate Version 1—and then create

Version 2. Continue this process until you have a Value Proposition and elevator speech you would be proud to share with anyone.

Value Proposition, Version 1:

_____

_____

_____

_____

Elevator Speech, Version 1:

_____

_____

_____

_____

_____

Value Proposition, Version 2:

_____

_____

_____

_____

Elevator Speech, Version 2:

_____

_____

_____

_____

The Ritz-Carlton was quick to hand me a card with their credo printed on it, and you should be prepared to do the same with your Value Proposition. It can be placed on either one or two sides of a wallet-size card, or it can be incorporated into the folded type of business card as shown in Figure 9.1.

If you are questioning the importance of an elevator speech, I respectfully refer you to the Fourteenth Dalai Lama. When asked about his religion, he replies, "My true religion is kindness." Now that's an elevator speech!

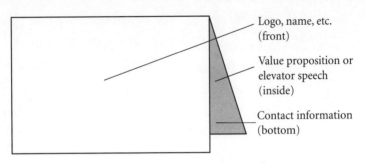

Logo, name, etc.
(front)

Value proposition or
elevator speech
(inside)

Contact information
(bottom)

FIGURE 9.1   Business card example.

TRANSFORMING YOUR ELEGANT
WORDS INTO REALITY

Can you imagine a Ritz-Carlton hotel handing out their credo card
and then neglecting the details that transform those elegant words
into reality? If they did, their credo would become a joke rather
than something to be admired. The bricks and mortar that transform your Value Proposition into a tangible reality is your ability to
deliver on all your promises and provide all the solutions expected.

We go to a doctor because we desire good health. When we call
for an appointment, we would like one right away, but that rarely
happens. When health problems arise, going to a specialist not
knowing what to expect is a troubling experience. The deluxe medical practice I referred to earlier has "proposed" solutions to both,
at a price. Imagine what would happen to the practice if someone
couldn't get a same-day appointment, couldn't reach them by cell
phone, or couldn't get their doctor to accompany them when visiting a specialist. Think for a moment about what it takes (behind
the scenes) to enable those doctors to provide this level of service.
That's where FedEx efficiency clicks into gear, and that requires
having the right people and processes in place.

HIRING THE RIGHT PEOPLE

Many salespeople who work with an affluent clientele discover that they need to hire people to assist them in delivering Ritz-Carlton service with FedEx efficiency. It is difficult, if not impossible, to do it alone. If you are committed to becoming affluent yourself, you may be required to dig into your pocket and invest in your business.

If you are in a situation where hiring a support person is possible, your goal must go beyond simply filling a slot. You do not want people who are looking for a job. Your path to success with the affluent is to build long-term relationships, and you cannot do that with today's typical job seeker. When you talk about your business and your goals, you need to carefully watch to see evidence that potential employees are becoming visibly excited about being part of that vision.

There are certain tasks associated with any position, and you must be certain that applicants have the attitudes, knowledge, abilities, experience, and skills to perform all of those tasks with a high level of competence. But that's just the beginning. The only people who will last in your Ritz-Carlton-level service environment are those with superior customer or client service skills. Here are the qualities you need to explore:

- *Caring:* They must care enough about providing extraordinary customer service that they will do whatever is necessary to provide it, either directly or by going out of their way to serve other employees at any level to help them serve a customer or client.
- *Friendly:* Being friendly when they are in the right mood, got a good night's sleep, and are being treated kindly by others is not sufficient. Their friendly attitude must weather almost any storm and shine through.
- *Attentive:* Everyone is attentive, but many focus that attention inward. You need people who are outwardly attentive,

constantly aware of other people's needs and looking for ways to meet those needs.

- *Energetic:* I see this as energy that is constantly moving toward the point of need. Some high-energy people never seem to focus, and that is not what you want.
- *Confident:* Confident people do not brag or fish for compliments. They simply step up and do what needs to be done. When complimented for it, they simply say, "Thank you," and keep doing it.
- *Never satisfied:* The three benchmarks of Ritz-Carlton-level service require people who are never satisfied. When this quality is combined with the other five, you have a person who will help you make things happen in a big way.

You can detect these qualities during a hiring interview. List each quality on the left side of a legal pad, leaving space between each for notes, then keep the following cues in mind:

- As you observe individuals during the interview, you will see indications that they are or are not *friendly, attentive,* and *energetic.* Write down the specific cues that you observe.
- To explore the *caring* quality, explain that caring for the needs of customers and other employees is an important aspect of the position they are seeking. Ask them to give you specific instances from previous jobs or other situations where they gave special care for customers, fellow employees, or other people. As they respond, make notes on what they did. Hold off evaluating what they say until later. If they overlook caring for customers and/or fellow employees, ask again for an example.
- To explore their *confidence,* give them examples of the kinds of tasks they will be performing if they are hired. Give them one example at a time and ask them how they would accomplish that task. Listen for and write down cues relating to their confidence level. Make special note of any comments

they make about "not being sure" or explaining the steps they would take to prepare for doing that task.

- Testing the *never satisfied* quality is challenging. Explain what you are currently doing in a specific area to meet the expectations of your customers or clients. Then ask them how they think this could be improved. After they have given you their suggestions, ask them if they would then be satisfied that they were doing everything they could to delight customers/clients. Note their response.

These methods aren't perfect, but they are far better than simply asking them how important each quality is or asking them whether they feel they have that quality. Giving them situations and then listening to and observing their response is a much better indication of reality.

KEEPING THE RIGHT PEOPLE

It's that long-term relationship with customers or clients issue again. If you've gone to the trouble to hire the right people, it only makes sense to work hard to keep them. Even in tough economic times when jobs are difficult to come by, people with the preceding qualities are highly valued. If you don't work hard to keep the right people, they will be the first to leave. The question is: What do you have to do to keep them? We tackle that question at two levels:

1. The *job context* level: These are the things that must be present to *prevent job dissatisfaction*. They include the following:
   - They must believe that their compensation and benefits are *adequate* enough for them to meet their personal and family financial obligations.
   - They must believe *equity* exists when they compare their compensation and benefits with what people in comparable positions receive—people within and outside the organization.

- They must believe there is *opportunity* for promotion within the organization to the level and types of positions to which they aspire.
- They must believe that the *expectations, support,* and *feedback* they receive from their immediate supervisor are fair, adequate, and consistent.

2. The *job content* level: These are the things that must exist in order to provide the *motivation to continually improve performance.* They include the following:
   - They must *believe in* and be *committed to* the *organization's purpose and goals.*
   - They must clearly see how what they do each day *contributes to achieving organizational goals.*
   - They must genuinely *enjoy performing the tasks* associated with their position.
   - They must have the *freedom to perform their tasks* without unnecessary interference from policies, procedures, rules, practices, and tight supervision.
   - They must have the *ability to reduce or eliminate* policies, procedures, rules, practices, and tight supervision that prevent them from successfully performing their tasks.
   - They must have an opportunity to *figure things out* and *make decisions.*
   - They must receive *adequate and ongoing training* that enables them to continually improve their performance.
   - *Risk taking* must be encouraged and rewarded, especially when they fail.

CREATING THE RIGHT PROCESSES

Processes tie individual tasks together, and they are especially important when different people perform those tasks. There are several things you must do to ensure that the right tasks are in place:

- Processes must always be *created* by the people who perform them, without exception. They can then be checked by legal and other specialists to ensure that they conform to important rules and regulations.

- Processes must also be *monitored and improved* by the people who perform them. Any improvements they make must be *recognized* and, when appropriate, *rewarded.*
- Processes must not be *changed* without the full participation and acceptance of the people who perform them.

IMPROVING PROCESSES THE RIGHT WAY

One of the Ritz-Carlton service benchmarks is, "Your actual level of service must extend beyond your minimum standard. Your customers or clients must be excited about what you are doing." The potential for achieving this level of services lies in your efforts to bring the people who perform interrelated tasks together periodically to look for ways to improve the established process that links those tasks together. Here is what they should look for:

- *Eliminate duplication:* Are any tasks being performed by two different team members or at different times in the process? Look especially for the same information being gathered or generated by different people, usually at different times.
- *Combine tasks:* Look for opportunities to take two different tasks and combine them, giving one individual the responsibility to perform them as a single task.
- *Simplify a task:* Discuss how each task is performed. Help the individual responsible for each task to find ways to simplify it, reducing the time required to perform it.
- *Eliminate a task:* Look for opportunities to eliminate one or more tasks that do not add value to the process. In other words, look for and get rid of "busy work."
- *Eliminate delays:* Look for paperwork that sits in someone's in-basket, waiting for attention. Figure out ways to make certain that when something arrives on anyone's desk, it is

handled within a certain time (set a performance standard) and then sent on without delay. This is especially important when prospects or clients are on the receiving end.

- *Checklists:* Look for opportunities to create checklists for use with repetitive tasks to reduce time and errors.
- *Errors:* After completing the preceding tasks, talk about any ongoing mistakes that have not yet been eliminated or things that continue to be overlooked. Determine what is causing each error, and then come up with ways to eliminate the cause.

This may not be the fun stuff to read about, but it is what makes coming to work every day meaningful and enjoyable. When you have great people who are clearly focused on serving customers or clients and working in an environment that is dynamic, challenging, and void of discouragement, you create the possibility of rising above the pack and convincing affluent customers or clients that you are different in the ways that matter.

SUMMARY

Ritz-Carlton has become the standard many of the affluent use for measuring the quality of the service they receive elsewhere. FedEx has created a similar standard for operational efficiency.

Your affluent customers or clients recognize that not everything is within your control, but they also expect you to compensate for any deficiencies. You need to accept personal responsibility for any service deficiencies that exist. You can do that by learning all you can about policies and procedures, building relationships with key service people, recognizing limitations, staying current with company changes, and following up periodically with every customer or client to identify and correct any problems.

You also need to do your homework to discover what your competitors are doing. Your objective is to determine which competitor is best-in-class and take steps to raise your own standards.

Research Facts

➤ Our 2004 APD Research identified seven criteria having influence over whether the affluent would use a suppler again:

1. Problems were resolved quickly and satisfactorily.
2. The supplier provided good service following the purchase.
3. The salespeople provided the information needed to make a satisfactory purchase decision.
4. The guarantee of satisfaction was clearly defined.
5. The customer's preferred brand was available through them.
6. The people who represented the supplier were friendly and helpful.
7. The supplier offered the lowest price available.

Ritz-Carlton employees carry a wallet-size credo with them. You need to develop a Value Proposition that communicates the benefits of doing business with you. To translate that Value Proposition into daily reality, you need to hire the right people and do everything you can to keep the right people. Then develop the right processes that tie individual tasks together to ensure that nothing falls through the cracks.

TAKING ACTION

- Use the checklist in this chapter to identify areas within your control where you can elevate your ability to provide Ritz-Carlton service and FedEx efficiency to affluent customers or clients.
- Use the secret shopper strategy to research your competitors and determine which are best-in-class in areas vital to your success. Use them as a benchmark to determine how you can improve.

- Develop your Value Proposition and your briefer elevator speech. Make certain that everyone at your location has a copy. Discuss it together, looking for ways to improve your efforts to provide the benefits that those statements promise.
- Upgrade your search, interviewing, and hiring practices to make certain that you have the right people.
- Because long-term relationships are so important, do everything you can to keep the right people.
- Make certain that you have the right processes in place. Use the seven techniques described in this chapter to continually improve those processes.

10

THE SECRET TO AFFLUENT LOYALTY

*Resolving any problems quickly and satisfactorily is the most signifi-
cant criteria for earning affluent loyalty that leads to future business.*

—FACTOID, 2004 APD RESEARCH

Ringgg. Ringgg. "Hello. Is this Mr. O-sha-lee?"

"Yes, but the name is pronounced Ox-lee."

"I'm sorry, Mr. Ox-lee—we have it in our records that you purchased a new entertainment center from XYZ Sound Systems last
week. Is that information correct?"

"Yes."

"Are you satisfied with the system you purchased from us?"

"It's okay, but I'm having trouble adjusting the surround sound
and figuring out the remote control."

"Oh. Well, on a scale of 10 high down to 1 low, how would you
rate the overall quality of the sound?"

"Like I said, I'm having trouble adjusting the surround sound
when I switch from music to watching DVDs."

"Oh. So, on a 1 to 10 with 10 being high . . ."

"Listen, I don't have time for these silly questions. Can you get
someone to help me get this surround sound working properly?"

"Mr. O-sha-lee, we're just a call center that has been contracted
by XYZ Sound Systems to conduct customer satisfaction surveys.
You will have to call XYZ Sound Systems directly."

"Okay." Click.

Customer satisfaction calls and survey forms have been used for
years by well-meaning companies and individuals who believe
they can rest easy once they know that you are satisfied with the
last transaction they had with you. That is a big mistake, because

it's based on the misconception that customer satisfaction equals customer loyalty. It does not, and here's why.

Satisfaction (or dissatisfaction) is a measure of how someone feels about a specific transaction, and about the only way to determine how someone feels is to ask him or her. Two weeks after having your car serviced, someone from the dealer calls and asks you a series of questions to see whether you are satisfied with their service. Even if you had been satisfied back then, you won't likely feel the same about the unanticipated interruption with a barrage of questions in the middle of your busy day. The service they provided was for *your* benefit; this phone call is for *their* benefit. What you will probably remember most in the future is how you felt about receiving that phone call. The same thing happens when you open an envelope and see a multipage survey form. That's why most of those survey forms end up in the trash.

It's important to understand that the customer/client satisfaction initiatives that companies use these days are considered smart business. But are they when they irritate the customer or client? What started years ago as a genuine effort to improve customer relations has evolved into a corporate beauty pageant that focuses primarily on promoting their business. Since 1968, J.D. Power and Associates has been using quality and customer satisfaction surveys for exactly that purpose. As stated in their advertising, "We represent the voice of the customer by translating survey responses into information that companies worldwide use to improve quality and customer satisfaction, as well as to help consumers make better decisions."

Granted, some quality and service issues will surface that need to be corrected, and most companies will quickly institute the requisite changes. But in today's world of media and hype, the real value lies in the promotional mileage that accompanies a high J.D. Power ranking. Advertising campaigns are built on this platform. Promotional materials proudly brand themselves around whatever customer service recognition and award that has been earned. Bonuses are often paid to employees on the basis of these awards. As an affluent salesperson focused on earning the loyalty of affluent clientele, you need to recognize all of this for what it is and be clear about the role you need to play. Here's an example.

Bob is a 15-year veteran financial advisor, and he has spent his entire career working for only one firm, which is somewhat unusual in the financial services world. Bob has lived through many changes, both within his firm and his industry.

A few years ago, Bob shifted his emphasis toward affluent clients. While doing a terrific job in attracting, servicing, and retaining affluent clients, Bob has also been reprimanded by his firm for having a poor client satisfaction rating, and that has cut into his annual bonus. Bob's corporate office commissioned, at considerable expense, an annual client satisfaction survey that is mailed to every client of the firm. As you might guess, Bob's affluent clients don't want to be bothered with surveys, and Bob is not about to follow his firm's guidelines and apply pressure to have them completed. The guidelines even tell him what he can say and do to entice his clients to give him high ratings.

Bob's firm is after J.D. Power and Associates' recognition. Bob is focused on earning the loyalty of his affluent clients and feels he cannot afford to waste time on what he considers to be a "manipulative survey."

Loyalty is a far more significant measure of the kind of relationship you have established with each customer or client. Loyalty defines what someone is, and it's measured by what he or she does over and over again. True customer loyalty prevails even when customers or clients have problems with your products or services from time to time, especially if the problem or mistake is handled quickly and effectively. A loyal customer or client emerges from an ongoing, carefully crafted, highly valued relationship. Loyalty is recognizable by these behaviors:

- Loyal customers or clients conduct business with you whenever the opportunity to do so arises.
- They tell you in direct and indirect ways that they plan to continue conducting business with you in the future.
- They welcome new strategies, solutions, products, and services that you recommend they consider.
- They resist the "pull" from your competition, and they tell you about it.
- They provide unsolicited introductions and referrals, and they gladly provide solicited introductions and referrals when you ask.

Ringgg. Ringgg.

"Good evening. XYZ Sound Systems, this is Barry speaking, can I help you?"

"This is Matt Oechsli—let me get right to the point. Remember that entertainment center you sold me last week?"

"I remember it well."

"I'm having problems getting the surround sound balanced. I know you're probably closing soon, but . . ."

"Mr. Oechsli (pronounced correctly), that is not a problem; I will stop by personally after we close. It will probably be within an hour. Will that work for you?"

"That would be great!"

"By the way, Mr. Oechsli, we will be introducing a new home office series next week, and I'd like to invite you to preview the series the day before we make it available to the general public. We're having a few valued clients in next Tuesday evening for a fully catered event, and I would love to have you join us. Is that possible?"

"Sure. I'll be there."

Now, that is the way to build customer loyalty!

Affluent customers and clients tend to be less tolerant with posttransaction efforts to find out how satisfied they are. In addition to being time crunched, their egos dictate that if you were doing your job, you should already know whether they are satisfied. The type of in-depth relationship you are establishing with them has a built-in feedback mechanism that lets you know in real time how things are. They are very demanding, and satisfying them is always a work in progress.

EARNING CUSTOMER OR CLIENT LOYALTY

The second call illustrates the level of commitment required to earn the loyalty of your affluent customers or clients. I have spent countless hours studying this issue and have concluded that there is no one set of activities that will garner affluent loyalty. However, here are seven principles that should shape your thinking and guide your efforts:

Seven Affluent Loyalty Principles

1. *Don't tell people about your service—show them.* Create a comfortable business atmosphere, on the phone, and especially in your physical place of business. Do not try to impress your affluent customers and clients with grandness. Instead, create an environment that is consistently courteous, professional, comfortable, and helpful. Many of today's affluent come from modest backgrounds. They are extremely busy and highly stressed and will not be impressed by unnecessary extravagance. They will be influenced by the help you give them as well as your attention to details—such as clean and functional restrooms, coffee rooms, and work areas.

2. *Practice hospitality by doing the little things.* Do not allow anyone else to greet your customers or clients. Be there yourself when they come in the door. Do not make them sit in front of a receptionist, waiting for you to get off the phone. Hold doors for people. When you are finished, walk your clients to the elevator, to the lobby, or even to their cars.

3. *Be available to affluent customers or clients 24 hours a day, even if you don't believe it's necessary.* Forget about normal

hours or the Monday through Friday atmosphere many business establishments typically project. On your personal literature, state something like, "Our office hours are whatever you need them to be." Continually verbalize this to your prospects and customers or clients.

4. *Enable customers or clients to make one call to get the answers.* Gather the people you work with and organize a customer or client response team. Distribute the responsibility to be on call among all your team members so that someone is available at all times. If you cannot possibly take these incoming calls yourselves, hire an answering service that will contact the available team member whenever a customer or client calls. When messages are left, the team member on call should respond immediately. Someone should be able to respond to a customer or client call within 15 minutes.

5. *Never say no.* When a customer or client asks, "Can you . . . ," the only answer you give is yes—even if you can't figure out immediately how to do what the customer or client wants. Obviously, this accommodation has some limits, but it's the mind-set that is most important. Be prepared to respond to *anything* a customer or client wants, regardless of what it is. Do not charge for these "extra" services unless it is absolutely necessary. If you must charge, discuss it with your customer or client ahead of time once you have determined what the cost will be. Will your affluent customers or clients take advantage of you? Rarely, and if a few do, it's worth it.

6. *Help customers or clients help you to provide Ritz-Carlton-level service.* There are simple ways you can do this. Explain every aspect of what you will be doing for your customer or client, step-by-step. When you go over your steps, consider the following four points:
   a. This is what I/we will be doing.
   b. These are the results you (the customer/client) can expect.

c. This is what I need you to do to help make this step successful.

d. This is the benefit you will receive from this step.

Next, tell the customer/client the best time to contact you: "You can contact me any time, day or night, but the best times are between _____ and _____ on _____." Finally, when customers and clients request something, tell them exactly *what information they need to provide* in order for you to help them in this specific area.

7. *Set a leadership example.* Take control of the relationship from the beginning. Do not expect your company, other team members, or service personnel to consistently exhibit the desired attitude and behaviors unless they *first* see them in you. Accept that you are the person responsible for affluent loyalty.

PROFESSIONAL PROBLEMS, SOLUTIONS, AND LOYALTY

The following case seems to break all the rules we have just laid out, but read it carefully. The affluent are strange creatures, and as soon as you think you really know how they think, they will throw you a curve. Or will they? They really do want to be loyal. Why? Because it makes their life easier. They want convenience, but they also want their problems solved. They are impatient but will wait like everyone else if they have to. Price is not a primary issue, but they are extremely price-value conscious.

Dr. Fellows was a magnet for patients. Even though he was the director of the local family medical practice that was a teaching facility for resident physicians, patients of all ages and incomes flocked into his waiting room, at times waiting hours for their appointment. Martin, a successful business owner, was one of his patients and a loyal follower who spread the good word about Dr. Fellows to anyone who would listen.

As so often is the case when dealing with matters of personal health, Martin's initial encounter with Dr. Fellows was an act of desperation. He was having serious problems with his left shoulder and had been to three different specialists and batteries of tests, but no one seemed to have a clue about how to solve his problem. That was until good old word-of-mouth influence entered the scene. One of Martin's trusted golfing buddies suggested that he schedule an appointment with Dr. Fellows. Apparently Dr. Fellows had made a very favorable impression when he helped the buddy's wife overcome her bout with tennis elbow.

Feeling as though he was grasping at straws (Martin hadn't been able to play golf for nearly a year), he contacted the family medical practice, which was a teaching facility that served mostly low-income families, and made an appointment with Dr. Fellows. Dr. Fellows diagnosed his problem immediately and started him on the path to recovery. A simple combination of physical therapy and anti-inflammatory medicine had Martin pain-free and back on the golf course within a month—which was about as long as it took Martin to get in to see Dr. Fellows.

Despite his affluence, Martin immediately set an appointment for his wife, Sally, at the family medical practice clinic when she began experiencing shortness of breath. He wanted her to be treated by Dr. Fellows. Only because of her husband's influence did she submit to having a complete physical with a strange (new) physician.

She was impressed with Dr. Fellows' bedside manner and his thoroughness but was not pleased with his diagnosis of her symptoms. Dr. Fellows was extremely concerned about the possibility of some serious artery blockage and recommended a complete exam with a cardiologist.

Sally refused, but not because she was in denial. There was no avoidance behavior due to her condition. After all, she felt ill enough to keep her initial appointment with Dr. Fellows. Her resistance revolved around insurance coverage or lack thereof. Her husband had sold his business, and they were in between insurance coverage, or at least that's what she assumed.

Dr. Fellows was adamant about the life and death implications (a severe heart attack was the risk) and applied all the pressure he felt was within his professional jurisdiction. It was to no avail. Despite her husband recently receiving millions of dollars from the sale of his business, Sally was not going to have a cardiologist examine her until she had insurance coverage, even when her life was at risk. She did, however, agree to schedule a follow-up appointment in four weeks with Dr. Fellows.

Interestingly, Sally had no problem paying for her visit with Dr. Fellows at a family medical clinic for low-income families. His reputation trumped any of her concerns over insurance coverage or the clientele of the clinic. Dr. Fellows had solved Martin's shoulder problem and, as far as Sally was concerned, successfully identified why she was short of breath. Both were now extremely loyal to him.

This case illustrates the truth of the results we found in our 2004 ADP Research regarding the important factors for the affluent in choosing medical and health services (see Table 10.1).

The visits to Dr. Fellows were definitely within Sally and Martin's budget. Both relied on recommendations of either an intimate

TABLE 10.1   Very important criteria for selecting medical and health services.

Criteria	Percent
Whether the provider and service is covered by our insurance.	65.2
What other sources say about the competence of the providers.	56.5
The total cost is within my/our budget.	53.8
What other sources say about the service provided.	52.6
Convenience, such as distance and easy access.	49.4

Source: APD Research Findings on Medical and Health Services, June 2004 research project, *How the Affluent Make Purchasing Decisions,* commissioned by the Oechsli Institute.

family member (husband) or a trusted friend (golfing buddy) to make their decision. Neither of them minded the inconvenience of the location, length of time to get an appointment, or the clinic atmosphere.

Although Sally was developing a loyalty to Dr. Fellows, she was not about to visit an unknown cardiologist, even when recommended by Dr. Fellows. She used insurance coverage as her excuse, but she knew how phony an excuse it was.

Loyalty is not something you manage. It is earned through the relationship you build over many encounters and transactions, or as in Dr. Fellows' case, the resolution of a serious problem. It is sustained to the degree that customers or clients or patients believe that you are committed to helping them, keeping them around, rather than driving them away.

SUMMARY

Many believe that customer satisfaction equals customer loyalty. It does not. Satisfaction simply measures how someone feels about a specific transaction.

Customer satisfaction calls and surveys were once a genuine effort to improve customer relations. Today, they have evolved into a corporate beauty pageant.

Research Facts

➤ Nothing is more important than your reputation; features and benefits, competence, problem solving, and service all have statistical significance to word-of-mouth influence.

➤ Being everything as advertised has the most impact in major purchase decision making.

➤ Cost has the least impact on affluent customer and client loyalty.

Loyalty defines what someone is, and it is measured by what they do over and over again. True customer loyalty prevails even when problems occur, especially if the problem is handled quickly and effectively. Loyal customers will do business with you again, welcome new products and services, resist the "pull" from your competition, and provide solicited and unsolicited introductions and referrals.

TAKING ACTION

- Memorize the seven loyalty principles.
- Develop an action plan with specific ways to implement each of those principles.
- Make certain you are everything that is expected and then some.
- Become a true problem solver.
- Become a servant to your clientele.

11

Maximizing Your Affluent Sales Opportunity

Affluent consumers with children living at home make up the largest single group that works over 60 hours per week.

—FACTOID, 2004 APD RESEARCH

As you read this chapter, you may begin to think I am trying to manipulate you into actually doing what I am suggesting you should do. You are absolutely right, which is why I suggest that you reread the factoid at the beginning of this chapter. It is a fact: Affluent consumers are extremely hard workers. They have put time and effort into their journey to affluence. How about you? Have you been putting the time in? Or should I ask: Are you willing to put the time in?

Even though I am confident you do not need to be reminded about the parallel paths I mentioned at the onset of this book, a gentle reminder is always a good thing. I am recommending that you look into the mirror and assess your commitment to affluence. At this point, it is of paramount importance that your commitment to affluence be total, your sleeves are rolled up, and you are working hard to progress down your parallel paths.

I hate to see the books I write just decorating people's bookshelves. I want to see those frayed edges, notes in the margins, and dirty fingerprint smudged covers. I write books for the same reason I agree to coach—to help people achieve more than they could if left to their own resources. So, please read on.

If you have read and thought about the content of the first 10 chapters, you know what it takes to maximize your affluent sales opportunity. The question is: What are you going to *do* with what you know? Another way of putting it is this: How will this new knowledge change your daily activity? This question may be more significant than you realize. When we conducted our initial research in 1999, we discovered 12 significant gaps between affluent investors' expectations and the performance of their financial advisor. Our most recent research, four-plus years later, indicates that not much has changed in the financial services industry—despite the fact that stockbrokers now call themselves *financial advisors* and many claim they are targeting the affluent market.

What you call yourself and whom you target doesn't matter much if you don't change what you do, especially when you have the research to show you what changes are required. The good news is that what the Cap Gemini Ernst & Young white paper (2002) called the mass affluent "underserved and untapped" investor market remains underserved and virtually untapped. So, what is the problem?

For many, what they do each day involves little more than reacting to the pressures and events of that day. Stephen Covey (1996) refers to this as getting caught up in "the tyranny of the urgent." It's what happens when you have a fuzzy future. As Yogi Berra so aptly put it, "If you don't know where you are going, you will wind up somewhere else." For daily activity to have significance and importance, it must be directly linked to a clearly defined future that you are working hard to create.

Wouldn't it be great if you could simply look into a crystal ball and see what the future has in store for you? Actually, you can—or nearly so. A crystal ball is clear, brilliant, and transparent. It draws you to gaze into it, see through it, and watch the future unfold before you.

To create your own crystal ball effect, you need to look within yourself and begin to imagine what *could be* if you effectively applied the ideas, strategies, and tactics contained in this book. This is what we call *envisioning your future*. My wife's experience with a new kitchen illustrates this point quite well.

Sandy, my wife of 26 years and counting, had been considering a new kitchen for a number of years. After getting a reference from a friend, Sandy discovered that the mother of one of our daughter's preschool friends worked at this "deluxe" new kitchen store as a salesperson or, as they referred to it, a kitchen consultant.

It had been at least 15 years since they had seen each other, so rather than call this acquaintance directly, she decided to begin her due diligence by visiting this deluxe new kitchen's web site. After a couple of visits to the site and some other preliminary research, she decided she liked what she saw on the deluxe new kitchen web site. She filled out the necessary contact information and clicked on the button to have a kitchen consultant contact her at their earliest convenience. She requested her old acquaintance by name.

If you have ever had your kitchen overhauled or have looked very closely into having a new kitchen installed, you know it is an expensive undertaking. Without being privy to the details, you could assume that a top-notch kitchen consultant working on commission could do very well—especially a kitchen consultant who had clear goals and was committed to maximizing his or her affluent sales opportunity. That is precisely why Sandy indicated her preference in kitchen consultants; she wanted to give the business to someone she knew.

Sandy was excited and let the entire family know about this upcoming project. I must admit that I wasn't looking forward to our kitchen being torn apart. Our old kitchen served my purposes, and a considerable outlay of cash was going to be required. So my approach was to listen, stay in the background, and get involved when the final purchase decision was about to be made.

Out-of-sight, out-of-mind, I forgot all about Sandy's kitchen project and her long-lost acquaintance until one day at the dinner table, in our old kitchen, she dropped a large envelope on my lap and announced that she finally heard from this deluxe new kitchen contractor. "I contacted this place over six months ago," she growled. "I asked for Susan's (our daughter's preschool friend) mother by name, and this is what I get with a business card of some other supposed kitchen consultant stapled to a letter saying how much they appreciate my interest in a new kitchen. They've got a lot of nerve."

The rest of the family, including me, had completely forgotten about her new kitchen project. After a few jokes from the kids about how long it would take them to build a new kitchen if it took over six months to send something in the mail and our daughter trying to recall whether her friend's mother actually worked at this deluxe new kitchen place, Sandy let us know that she had heard enough, and we all let the subject drop. At the time of this writing, it appears that Sandy has also dropped the idea of having a new kitchen.

It was obvious that none of the salespeople at this "deluxe" new kitchen was very goal focused. It wasn't as though my wife went into the black hole of cyberspace. She got a response, but it was just a little late. I would expect any goal-focused kitchen consultant or affluent salesperson whose company had a web site that fielded inquiries to be racing every morning to be the first salesperson to check the e-mail. In fact, I would expect the company to have procedures for processing these web site solicited inquiries. Neither appeared to be the case in this instance.

ENVISIONING YOUR FUTURE

So what does envisioning your future really mean? Exactly what you'd expect. To *envision* means to imagine something that does not yet exist. It answers the question: "What quality of business and personal life do I want 12 months from now?" John Ruskin said that "quality is never an accident; it is always the result of intelligent effort." If 12 months from now your business and personal life are not what you want, the culprit will be a lack of intelligent effort—not all those external factors we tend to blame.

The whole purpose of this book is to help you define the "intelligent effort" required to maximize your affluent sales opportunity, but knowing what to do is not enough. You must also be clear about why it's important to refocus your daily activity. That's why it's critical that you begin by envisioning your future.

Envisioning what your business and personal life will look like 12 months from now is best accomplished when you do two things:

1. *Contrast* where you are now with where you want to be in 12 months, so that the gap between *now* and *want to be* will be clear.
2. *Avoid becoming concerned* with how you will close the gap between now and 12 months from now. Be confident that if you can envision your future, you can achieve it.

Selecting what you will contrast is important. It should be those items that will help you define the daily activities required to close the gap, making you feel as though you are being pulled toward your desired future each time you tackle and complete a particular goal-focused activity. Each item should be measurable so that each week you can clearly define how far you have come and how far you still need to go. Each gap you create becomes a "work in progress." The most obvious items are these:

*   Average monthly sales
*   Number of affluent customers/clients
*   Average monthly income

Think about how these three items are interrelated. Be honest about the numbers you are achieving *now*. Select challenging, but realistic numbers when stating where you want to be in 12 months. With those numbers in place, select other measurable items that you know will be important aspects of building your business. For example:

*   Average weekly introductions and referrals to affluent prospects
*   Average number of affluent prospects you are actively pursuing

- Memberships in "one with the affluent" organizations
- Number and types of activities and events you will attend to place yourself in the path of affluent people you want to attract
- Number of affluent names and e-mail addresses in your database
- Average number of e-mail promotions sent each month

Not all of the items you include have to come from this book, but each item should be measurable, and you should be convinced that each item will serve to pull you toward where you want to be 12 months from now.

If you have set the goals you want to achieve and you have clearly defined the gap you must close to achieve them, your next step is to determine what you must do to close it.

CLOSING THE GAP

Whatever you presently do every day, whether you believe it's effective or not, you do out of habit. Experts tell us that 80 percent of how we think and what we do is "habit driven." Habits are formed over time and become stored in our subconscious mind, eliminating the need to stop and think everything through every time. We simply do it out of habit.

Mental habits shape our attitudes. *Doing habits* emerge as behavioral patterns that define and drive our actions. Over time, what we repeatedly think and do out of habit becomes comfortable, creating what we often refer to as our *comfort zone*. The extent to which you are able to break out of your comfort zone and use new knowledge to shape new attitudes and behavioral patterns will determine the answer to the "How will this new knowledge change your daily activity?" question. Most critical is the behavioral pattern that emerges from all this. Will it be an *avoidance pattern* or an *achievement pattern*?

Let's assume that you want very much to capitalize on what you have learned in this book and use it to achieve the future you have just defined. Which of the following patterns best describes how you will go about doing that?

- You go back through the book and start rereading the sections that you believe are most important so you will understand them better. As you study that material, you make notes about how you need to prepare to implement the *how-to* parts of the book. You focus that preparation on tasks such as researching the organizations you might want to join to become "one with" the affluent of your community, how you will create the kind of affluent sales environment described in Chapter 3, the steps you need to take to put social self-consciousness behind you, setting up your e-mail database, writing your Value Proposition, writing and memorizing scripts for introductions and referrals—and the list goes on. As you read and write, you are aware that feelings of doubt arise now and then. At those points, you simply stop for a while and do other things until those feelings go away.

- You set three goals to be completed by the end of next week. The first goal is to identify and initiate a face-to-face encounter with three affluent prospects. The second goal is to select and join an organization that meets two criteria: You believe in its purpose and goals, and joining will enable you to immediately begin the process of becoming one with the affluent of your community. The third goal is to initiate three to five changes in your sales environment that will bring it closer to becoming the affluent sales environment you want. You write down the specific steps required to achieve each goal by next Friday and schedule those steps as fixed daily activities (FDAs) in your day planner. Finally, you begin working on those activities immediately, determined to complete at least three of them before the end of the day.

Which of these two scenarios would you label an *avoidance pattern*? An *achievement pattern*? Which best describes what your natural tendency would be toward implementing what you have learned from this book? Even more important, which describes what you will do?

ACTIVATING YOUR ACHIEVEMENT CYCLE

Have you ever discovered that there's a devilish little voice of doubt following you around: "I can't pull this off." "I don't know anyone who is affluent." "I'm not sure what I would say if I were introduced to an affluent person." "They'd see right through me." "What do I have to offer that they aren't already getting from someone else?" This little voice begins to speak to you soon after establishing your goals as you begin thinking about what it will take to close the gap and get there. There is a cure, or an antidote to be more accurate. It begins with understanding the garbage-in, garbage-out impact those thoughts can have on your behavior.

In his book, *The Self-Talk Solution* (1988), Dr. Shad Helmstetter explains: "One of the most important discoveries in recent years has been the role our own casual thinking plays in shaping of our lives" (p. 14). Neuroscientists have discovered that thoughts are electrical impulses that trigger both electrical and chemical reactions in the brain. The impact is significant, whether those thoughts are good or bad. Negative thinking doesn't simply result in continued negative thinking. It also stimulates negative behavior, and that's when it becomes serious.

What we do is driven by three components: feeling, thinking, and doing. When we allow negative feelings to emerge from our subconscious and shape our thinking, it results in the "I can't pull this off" mind-set described earlier, and we begin to find excuses for not doing what we know deep down inside we should do. We have allowed those negative feelings to lead to thinking that produces inactivity and allows us to remain within our comfort zone.

Activating your achievement cycle can reverse that process because it changes the sequence to doing—thinking—feeling. Doing is goal-driven and is almost completely under your control. That's how you break out of your comfort zone—by doing activities that are linked to a goal. Regardless of how you feel and what you are thinking, keep the goals you want to achieve in front of you and simply do what you know you have to do. Once your goals are set and the gap you must close to achieve them becomes clear, you are ready to activate your achievement cycle.

ACHIEVEMENTS OF THE PAST

What is fascinating to me is how this achievement cycle is instinctive to the human species. In fact, you have engaged this cycle in the past—everyone has. Probably the most significant difference between mediocrity and high levels of achievement is that high achievers consistently reactivate their achievement cycle whereas the average salesperson, that poor soul who is always struggling to make it into the next income bracket but keeps falling short, activates his or her achievement cycle infrequently.

Let's revisit a big hairy audacious goal that you set for yourself, and somehow, someway, you made it happen. You achieved your goal. The odds are that this achievement did not make you rich or famous, but I guarantee it followed a predictable pattern. It is the reactivation of this pattern that is going to lead you to affluence. Can you recall the goal? I'll bet it sends chills down your spine just thinking about it. I would also wager that in recounting this major accomplishment in your past, you can remember being pulled far outside your comfort zone in your efforts to achieve it.

I remember setting a goal to write my first book. Not ever having written a book, all of this was a new experience for me. Do you think all my thoughts were positive about the prospects of writing this book? Hardly! I had that little devilish voice of doubt whispering sweet bromides in my ear to the tune of, "Who's going to want to read anything you write?" As far as my feelings were concerned, my self-image and self-esteem were light-years away from that of a writer. I felt like a fraud, a pretender, a wanna-be, hoping that nobody would find me out.

For some reason, my goal of writing a book had been imprinted into my mind, and even though I heard the devilish voice of doubt trying to sabotage my efforts, I proceeded to write anyway. Despite the fear of being a fraud, I forged ahead. A little over 18 months later, I was the proud author of my first published book. Achieving this goal did not make me famous or rich, but it epitomized this achievement cycle, the same cycle you are revisiting through recalling your past goal accomplishments.

The secret is to understand that the power of this cycle comes by reactivating it over and over again. Let's use your affluent sales goals as the context. Here's how it works:

Goal Commitment: Subconscious Imprinting

- *Envision your future* following the process outlined earlier in this chapter.
- *Repeat your goals* at the beginning of each week and daily if it will help. Write them down and say them over and over. Even if you have memorized them, read them at the beginning of each week. Refine them if you feel the need.
- *Visualize your goals* by sitting back, relaxing, and seeing yourself successfully going through the steps required to achieve each goal. Notice how great you feel as a result, and you will begin to block those negative feelings of doubt that seem to emerge from nowhere:

Goal-Focused Action Steps

- *Define FDAs* that you must perform to achieve your goals. You may not have to perform each activity each day, but you must be performing specific activities daily. That's why we call them fixed daily activities—to emphasize the importance of doing important, goal-achieving activities each and every day.

- *Plan, schedule, perform, and measure* weekly. *Plan* at the beginning of the week what FDAs you will do each day. *Schedule* those FDAs in your day planner. *Perform* the FDAs scheduled each day, noting how good it feels to check each one off. *Measure* what you accomplished at the end of the week, noting how you are being systematically pulled toward your goals and how good that feels.

Stepping up and digging into that first FDA is always the toughest. As you progress from activity to activity, day by day, week after week, it gets easier. The activities don't get easier, but your ability to perform them and achieve desired results does. There are three reasons for that, and each begins with a "C":

1. *Conviction* is believing without proof. That's what you must do from the very outset. You must be convinced that the goals you set are both believable and achievable. You must be convinced that if you do the hard work, venture outside your comfort zone, and perform your FDAs, you can achieve your goals. When conviction is lacking, I see lots of finger pointing at company policies, poor management, down markets, and anything else that will provide an excuse for inactivity. Look at the future you have envisioned. Put the excuses aside and believe without proof. As you take that step and each subsequent step, your confidence will grow.

2. *Confidence* is either the pillar or killer of success. Confident people don't sit around thinking and talking about it. They get up and go do it. Too much thinking can create the *avoidance pattern* we described in the first scenario earlier in this

chapter. The most effective way to build confidence is by doing FDAs that are directly linked to a serious goal. You then become:

- Convinced that your goals are the right ones.
- Confident to take your next step toward your goals.
- Confident that you have the expertise to take the next step.
- Confident that taking that next step will not only advance you toward your goals but also enable you to gain the additional expertise and added confidence to take the next step.

   As your confidence grows, your competency grows right along with it.

3. *Competence* evolves from experience, not by taking classes or reading books. Knowledge produces competence only when you use it, make mistakes, adjust, and then find ways to do it better. That's why face-to-face encounters with the affluent are critical. They create experiences that enable you to learn, gain confidence, and become more competent. Competency is also the product of doing the right things, and experience is again the only true determinant of what those right things are.

You have probably figured this out by now, but the key is in doing the activities that are linked to your goal even when that little devilish voice is whispering, "You can't pull this off." It means doing your FDAs even when you don't feel like doing them and start thinking of other (more comfortable) things you could do. All people can do what they need to do when they feel like doing it. If that was all it took to achieve a goal, everyone would be a success. But it is not.

Once you are convinced you have the right goals and are actively pursuing them one FDA step at a time, your confidence will grow, your competence will steadily improve, you will become one with your affluent clientele, and soon you, too, will be affluent. There is simply no other way.

STAYING ON YOUR CRITICAL PATH

The Critical Path was the subtitle of one of my earlier books on selling. It evolved from a project planning and management technique that came into prominence in the 1960s. The idea is to focus on critical activities that must be done each day—activities so vital to your success that failure to do them will significantly delay your progress. It also serves as an activity filter. There are many activities you could engage in on a given day. Compare the *avoidance pattern* activities with the *achievement pattern* activities at the beginning of this chapter, and you will see what I mean. What you need to focus on is critical path-type activities—those described in the second scenario, not the first.

The critical path concept can also serve as an activity accelerator. The key is to monitor your critical path-type activities on a weekly basis, enabling you to monitor your progress and make adjustments quickly. The Critical Path ORGANIZER illustrated on pages 192 through 195 has been developed to facilitate this process. When using the organizer, follow these guidelines:

- *Plan your week.* There are seven categories of face-to-face contacts (page 192). Your goal should be to make a set number of contacts of some type each day. In the spaces provided, enter the names of the people you hope to contact followed by the contact code (see the bottom of the page).
  —Second, complete the Prospect TRACKING section (page 193). This is your opportunity to review not only how many prospects you have in your pipeline but also their potential—and your strategy for transforming that prospect into a customer or client.
  —Next, set targets for how many contacts you will make in each category and record those numbers on your Weekly Prospecting SCORECARD (see bottom of page 193).
  —Finally, make a list of Business Builder Activities, Affluent Sales Environment Activities, and Family & Health Activities in your Weekly Activity SCHEDULER (pages 194–195).

Critical Path ORGANIZER

Week of ___/___/___ to ___/___/___

Face-To-Face Contacts
Activity Drives The Dream!

Activity	Type of Contact	Objective	Type of Contact
Customer/Client Retention Contacts		**Objective: Retain Key Customers/Clients**	
Customer/Client Upgrade Contacts		**Objective: Introduce New Products/Services**	
Customer/Client Networking		**Objective: Arrange Introductions & Referrals**	
One With Them **Activities & Events**		**Objective: Identify Potential Prospects**	
Affluent Prospect – Introductions		**Objective: Attract New Prospects**	
Affluent Prospect – Referral Contacts		**Objective: Attract New Prospects**	
Affluent Prospect – Placing Myself in their Path		**Objective: Attract New Prospects**	

Type of Contact: P = Phone Call   E = Email   M = Scheduled Meeting   S = Social Event

Your Critical Path to Affluent Selling Success

Prospect TRACKING

| [1]Status: | C = Current | N = New this week |

	Name	[1]Status	[2]Potential	[3]Strategy
1				
2				
3				
4				
5				
6				
7				
8				
9				
10				
11				
12				
13				
14				
15				
16				
17				
18				

[1] C = Current
N = New this week

[2] Brief description of their interest in what you offer.

[3] Brief description of steps you plan to take this week to transform this prospect into a customer or client.

Weekly Prospecting SCORECARD

Transfer from the first page.

CUSTOMER/CLIENT Contacts	Target	Actual
• Retention Contacts	_____	_____
• Upgrade Contacts	_____	_____
• Networking Contacts	_____	_____

ORGANIZATIONAL Contacts	Target	Actual
• *One With Them* Activities & Events	_____	_____

PROSPECT Contacts	Target	Actual
• Affluent Prospect – Introductions	_____	_____
• Affluent Prospect – Referral Contacts	_____	_____
• Affluent Prospect Contacts – From Placing Myself in their Path	_____	_____

The Oechsli Institute, 1005 Battleground Ave., Greensboro NC 27408
(800) 883-6582 • matt@oechsli.com • www.oechsli.com

Weekly Activity SCHEDULER

Monday _____	Tuesday _____	Wednesday _____	Thursday _____
7 _____	7 _____	7 _____	7 _____
8 _____	8 _____	8 _____	8 _____
9 _____	9 _____	9 _____	9 _____
10 _____	10 _____	10 _____	10 _____
11 _____	11 _____	11 _____	11 _____
12 _____	12 _____	12 _____	12 _____
1 _____	1 _____	1 _____	1 _____
2 _____	2 _____	2 _____	2 _____
3 _____	3 _____	3 _____	3 _____
4 _____	4 _____	4 _____	4 _____
5 _____	5 _____	5 _____	5 _____
6 _____	6 _____	6 _____	6 _____
7 _____	7 _____	7 _____	7 _____
8 _____	8 _____	8 _____	8 _____
9 _____	9 _____	9 _____	9 _____
Phone/email/fax:	Phone/email/fax:	Phone/email/fax:	Phone/email/fax:
✓	✓	✓	✓

		Other Activities TO SCHEDULE
Friday _____	**Saturday** _____	**Business Builder Activities**
7 _____		
8 _____		
9 _____		
10 _____		
11 _____		
12 _____		
1 _____		**Affluent Sales Environment Activities**
2 _____		
3 _____		
4 _____	**Sunday** _____	
5 _____		
6 _____		
7 _____		
8 _____		
9 _____		**Family & Health Activities**
Phone/email/fax:	Phone/email/fax:	

- *Plan each day.* Enter the contacts and activities for that day in your Weekly Activity SCHEDULER (pages 194–195). Then add all your other time-driven FDAs for that day. You should meet first thing in the morning with your support staff to review the previous day and to preview the FDAs for the day. Ask whether there is anything they need from you, and then make certain you provide whatever they need. This is the best way I know to go from being reactive to proactive.
- *Measure your weekly activity.* At the end of each week, record in your Weekly Prospecting SCORECARD the actual number of contacts you made in each of the seven categories.
- *Analyze your weekly activity.* First, review the target versus actual numbers under your Weekly Prospecting SCORECARD.
  —Where and why were you under target—over target?
  —What progress have you made with each of your prospects?
  —How effectively did you perform with each of your contacts?
  —What changes do you want to make next week to improve your performance?

You will discover that the thought process and discipline that this Critical Path ORGANIZER brings to your business development efforts far outweigh the time required to plan, record, and analyze the information it generates. If you would like to download a copy to use, this form is available to you at no cost. Visit: www.oechsli.com/cp-org.

SUMMARY

The question now is: What are you going to do with what you have learned?

The first step in answering that question is to look forward 12 months and envision the future that you want to exist at that point. This will enable you to refocus your daily activity toward accomplishing what is important to you.

Envisioning your future is best accomplished by contrasting where you are now with where you want to be. That way, the gap between where you are now and where you want to be becomes clear.

Whichever items you include in your plan, you need to be convinced that each will serve to pull you toward where you want to be 12 months from now.

The next question focuses on what you will do to close the gaps you envisioned. Will your activities take the shape of an avoidance pattern or an achievement pattern? You shape your daily activities into an achievement pattern when, instead of letting your negative and fear-driven feelings pull you off track, you instead focus on doing. You do those FDAs that need to be done, regardless of what you are thinking or how you are feeling.

Stepping up and digging into that first FDA is always the toughest. Conviction is where to begin. You must believe that your goals are both believable and achievable. As you perform those activities, your confidence builds. As you gain more experience, your competence grows.

It is not a coincidence that affluence and hard work go hand in hand. The work is usually multifaceted: actual hours on the

---

Research Facts

➢ Nearly three-quarters, 72.2 percent, of the affluent in our study are married with children living at home or away from home. These are typically the hardest workers and, on average, put in over 60 hours a week.

➢ Of those in the study, 22.4 percent have worked their way into affluence as business owners, and 25.9 percent are self-employed professionals. However, the largest single grouping, 44.9 percent, of affluence was located in the salaried and commissioned employee category—your world. Only 0.6 percent inherited their affluence.

job, hours spent solving problems and handling service issues, and hours invested continually mastering a craft. The vast majority work far more hours than people who are not committed to affluence.

TAKING ACTION

- Envision your future following the process outlined in this chapter.
- Repeat your goals at the beginning of each week and daily if it will help. Write them down and say them over and over.
- Visualize your goals by sitting back, relaxing, and seeing yourself successfully going through the steps required to achieve each goal.
- Define the FDAs that you must perform to achieve your goals.
- Plan, schedule, perform, and measure those FDAs on a weekly basis.
- Make certain you are working both hard and smart, replicating the work ethic of the affluent in our study.

12

THE 12 COMMANDMENTS OF AFFLUENT SELLING

It is essential that the product and service you offer is everything the affluent expects—and more than you advertised.

—FACTOID, 2004 APD RESEARCH

M y sole objective in the sequence and content of the previous 11 chapters was to provide you with an up-to-date road map to success in selling to the affluent, one that is based on the most recent research available on the affluent consumer and how they make purchasing decisions. Applied properly, this information is designed to serve as a blueprint to help you not only sell effectively to the affluent but also achieve affluence in your own right. It might be helpful to remind yourself periodically that 44.9 percent of our 2004 APD Research respondents earned their affluence as salaried employees and commissioned salespeople. There can be no doubt that you are in the right profession for acquiring affluence.

Some readers will simply cherry-pick a handful of the gems from these chapters and thereby improve their affluent selling skills and increase their earnings. That is obviously a good thing. However, there will be others who will diligently commit to becoming affluent by systematically applying all of these principles. I have created the 12 commandments with the hope of getting some of the cherry-pickers to dig deeper and to provide those of you who are totally committed to affluence with a series of simple reminders to help accelerate your progress. Our entire 2004 APD Research is boiled down into 12 small nuggets, reminders that are short on verbiage and long on meaning.

Whenever I am engaged in a project of this nature, I get a nagging concern about my ability to communicate my message in a succinct, user-friendly manner. I must confess: That is how I am feeling now. I am concerned that I may have distracted you, given you too many pieces of information to digest, engaged you in an exercise that has pulled you off your critical path, or simply confused you somewhere along the way. So, if you got derailed in Chapter 5 over the concept of *becoming one with the affluent* or stuck back in Chapter 4 wrestling with *social self-consciousness,* I will rest easy knowing that I helped you get back on track by summarizing key points into these 12 gems.

The following 12 commandments for success in selling to the affluent are a simple prompting, a compilation of everything you have read condensed into key concepts. At times I have changed the verbiage, but at all times you will find references to the specific chapters that can help you master a particular commandment. Are these the only commandments? No, of course not. However, they do make sense to me, and they make me feel better about presenting all of this information. It is my hope that these commandments will further assist you in mastering the art of selling to the affluent.

COMMANDMENT 1: BE TOTALLY COMMITTED

Selling your products or services to the affluent is not a job that will reward you handsomely if you exert only a halfhearted effort. You will not be able to become one of the elite earners by faking sincerity and simply going through the motions. You might think this goes without saying, but my 20-plus years of working with professional salespeople suggest that this point must be continuously reinforced. *Total commitment* is listed first here because it forces you to be front and center. You must become one with the affluent in order to fulfill your potential when selling to the affluent, and that requires total commitment.

If you were to take everything that I have covered in the preceding chapters and boil it down into one word, it would be *commitment.* Without commitment, you cannot and will not consistently perform the tasks necessary for affluent sales success. Commit to yourself and to your career. Believe in both regardless of what anyone tells you—whether family members, friends, colleagues, or your sales manager. Nothing can replace your passion, that sheer force of positive energy you bring to your profession. You must love your job and trust your passion to excel in your career.

But, being totally committed involves more than simply loving your job. Total commitment is the fuel that inspires you to work hard and work smart. It provides you with the personal power that inspires trust, makes you believable, and increases your magnetic pull in affluent circles. It serves as the motivation behind all the learning and professional development you have undertaken and will continue to pursue. Commitment is the tonic that helps drown out that devilish voice of doubt and keeps you doing what needs to be done when you feel like doing something else. All true greatness is born out of total commitment.

Everyone loves a winner. The hard-working and self-made people, who accounted for over 90 percent of our 2004 APD Research respondents, love to encounter people cut from the same cloth. When your affluent customers and clients see you as a highly committed professional who is both responsive to their needs and goal focused, they will respond positively to you. But, they must sense that you are real and comfortable in your own skin. Nobody likes a phony.

When you get right down to it, all personal development stems from a commitment that is shaped by reality. For example, few people are healthy and fit just because they are blessed with good genes. Granted, genes play a role in who we are, but the vast majority of healthy and fit people are real about their health, have made a personal commitment to it, have made an honest assessment of their current state of affairs, work at it, and have developed healthy lifestyle habits, both attitudinal and behavioral. As a result, they eat better, exercise regularly, are moderate in their consumption of alcohol, and are careful to get their sleep.

Being real about your career and committed to being one with the affluent is no different. You cannot excel in your career by selling to the affluent from the sidelines, sitting back and waiting for them to come to you. You must be committed to finding them. If that means overcoming any hesitations or social self-consciousness, you need to reread Chapter 4 and work through the exercises that will enable you to overcome this internal barrier. To master the art of selling to the affluent, you must become part of who they are and what they do. If you have any questions about what it means to become one with the affluent, visit Chapter 5. Review the questions I ask there, the civic organizations that are listed, and the preparation steps for getting involved. If you are truly totally committed, you will find that none of this is very difficult.

Here is the reality. Whenever you are face-to-face with prospective affluent customers or clients, whether in your office or at your chamber of commerce, if you are not totally committed, you risk being perceived as a pretender. You will not be selling out if you change how you dress or become involved in a bit of social climbing, as long as you are true to who you are and clear about where you are going. Linking goals to acquiring affluence is what your affluent customers, clients, and prospects have experienced on a personal level. They understand. Quite possibly, at some stage in their lives, they refined their skills, expanded their knowledge, and upgraded their status by a committed effort. So must you.

COMMANDMENT 2: BE AS ADVERTISED

Do you recall the last time you purchased an item or paid for a professional service that was not all that it claimed to be? I certainly do, and it makes me angry just thinking about it.

We had outgrown our offices and decided to purchase a small office building not far from my home. If you have ever moved an office, you know that it is one major hassle after another. In our case, we decided to upgrade our phones, phone service, and DSL Internet connection at the same time. We received a recommendation from a colleague, contacted the company, and met with their sales representative. Everything seemed to go well. The phone lines were installed in a timely manner; all the technology for our network and DSL lines was up and running on schedule. We were assured that we had a system that would serve our needs in the present and well into the future. At that moment, we were satisfied customers.

Months later, that all changed. As our database grew, our e-mail usage increased significantly. We also initiated a new e-mail newsletter format that increased the size of each e-mail we were sending. These changes created immediate problems. A simple newsletter that previously required one day to send was now taking over a week. Inquiries from clients and readers, along with a survey we were conducting, were clogging our system. Basically, our technology was grinding to a slow halt, and we needed to figure out what was wrong.

Our initial phone service salesperson had assured us that we were doubling our broadband capacity, which, according to him, would be more than adequate for our needs. Frustrated, I pulled the file and called the salesperson, only to discover that he was no longer with the company. I was transferred to another salesperson, who pulled our file, listened to me describe our problem, and then informed me that we did not have enough bandwidth to accomplish all that we were trying to do. In fact, I discovered that we had less bandwidth with them than we had before switching. Ouch!

When the new sales rep heard this, she proceeded to lecture me about reading my monthly statements where everything is spelled out in "black and white." I had heard enough and requested her supervisor. The supervisor not only failed to resolve my problem but also claimed she could not, or would not, do anything about the dishonesty (at least from my perspective) of charging us more, telling us we were getting increased broadband capacity, and then delivering less than we had in the first place. We have now ordered another new phone and DSL line system—a system with significantly more bandwidth at about the same cost.

The former salesperson told us we would receive more bandwidth from them and that it would be adequate for our future needs. Not being as advertised and having a "buyer beware" attitude not only caused this carrier to lose our business but also ensured that other businesses will hear about it—in a community where the word spreads quickly. On top of all of that, they have helped to create suspicion of the entire industry. We have made our new provider jump through every conceivable hoop, with warranties and guarantees in writing. They have responded admirably, but I must admit that we remain skeptical.

Recall what happened to Cadillac's reputation in the mind of luxury car owners when manufacturing cut corners on the production of a true luxury product, but the marketing department went all out promoting the product as a new and improved luxury automobile. Because the product did not measure up to its advertising image, GM's sales and reputation suffered. Detroit is now struggling to regain the luxury car market share that they lost to their Japanese and European competitors. Who would have ever considered a Japanese luxury car over Cadillac 30 years ago?

The financial services industry is currently facing its version of what Detroit has had to deal with. Scandals and corporate malfeasance aside, all eight criteria in our 2004 APD Research relating to the selection of a primary financial coordinator showed statistically significant gaps between affluent investor expectations and the performance of their current financial advisor. However, glance at any of the advertising of the major financial services firms, and you will quickly see how these marketing departments are suggesting the opposite when it comes to their advisors.

This is very good news for any financial professional or firm who is willing to take the necessary steps to ensure that their affluent clientele will receive a consistent experience that is congruent with their firm's advertising message. If a major securities firm is advertising wealth management services and suggesting that their financial advisors are capable of overseeing all of the financial affairs for the affluent, their financial advisors must be as advertised. If they are not, credibility and trust are damaged. If that failure continues for long, serious market share will be lost. Just ask Detroit!

Further highlighting this point, although 40.9 percent of our survey respondents said they were not interested in having a "go-to" financial coordinator, it was clear from their other responses that they wanted exactly the kinds of solutions that a financial coordinator would provide. This suggests a phenomenal opportunity, but the current reality is that the affluent do not think, at least according to the responses in our 2004 APD Research, that bank reps, financial advisors, stockbrokers, or insurance agents are capable of acting in this capacity.

Be as advertised, be real, have the features and benefits you promise, and be consistent, and you will develop a reputation and a brand that will be magnetic.

COMMANDMENT 3: BE A PROBLEM SOLVER

We do not live in a perfect world, and nobody is more acutely aware of this reality than your affluent customers, clients, and prospects. They are business owners, self-employed professionals, executives, and commissioned salespeople who have to deal with Murphy's Law all the time. What they do expect, and insist on, is that any problem they might incur, no matter how big or small, be resolved quickly and to their satisfaction. You, as their salesperson and first line of contact, are the person who must make certain that all problems are solved in this fashion.

I fully understand that you did not sign on with the service department. You are in the world of high commissioned sales. But it is you, not the service department, who will be earning the commissions on the repeat business that is generated as a result of being a first-class problem solver. Being a problem solver will also benefit you far beyond repeat business, for a solved problem is the high octane fuel that propels word-of-mouth influence.

When it comes to major purchase decisions, affluent consumers will remember and talk about the problems they encountered. Resolve them quickly and to their satisfaction, and they will sing your praises. Fail to do that, and you can expect the kind of reactions that resulted from Bob and Mary's sports car fiasco back in Chapter 2. Bob was telling his story, spreading negative word-of-mouth influence, to anyone who would listen.

Be a problem solver and your reputation will be on the road to becoming the brand of choice within your market.

COMMANDMENT 4: BE A SERVANT

There is more to repeat business and word-of-mouth influence than being a problem solver. Problem solving alone will get you only so far. But making a personal commitment to provide the level of Ritz-Carlton service that was discussed in Chapter 9 will take you the rest of the way. It's the combination of being a servant and a problem solver that will enable you to maximize the value of repeat business and word-of-mouth influence. It continues to fascinate me that even though first-class service is expected by the affluent, providing it differentiates you from your competitors. Excellent service is greatly appreciated, remembered, and talked about.

There are many factors going into this anomaly, one being that service has become so shoddy that anyone excelling in this area will stand out. Another factor is the high level of stress that most affluent consumers cope with on a daily basis. If you, by providing extraordinary service, act as a small respite from the craziness, you will be especially appreciated and remembered.

Combining Commandments 3 and 4 will give you a foolproof recipe for branding. Word-of-mouth influence will become the heart and soul of your business growth. Sprinkle in the other ingredients (or commandments), and you will find yourself in the fast lane to personal affluence.

COMMANDMENT 5: BE A TRUSTED SOURCE OF INFORMATION

The affluent are confident in their decision-making ability and will search diligently for the information they need to make buying decisions, especially major buying decisions. You cannot provide all the information they need to decide about the types of products and services you offer, but you must be a source of information that they can trust. They are smart enough to know when a given information source is lacking or misleading. But, once they discover that they can really trust you, they will be drawn to you like a magnet. And because they don't have time to waste, you will have a distinct advantage, assuming that you made the effort to attract them to you in the first place.

It is essential that you know your products and services in depth and that you learn as much as you can about your competitors' offerings. In Chapter 7, we emphasized that a qualified prospect is one who is experiencing or feeling dissatisfaction about something your products and services can fix. We also suggested that you create a product and service profile that describes in detail the features, advantages, solutions, and evidence of each product and service you offer. If your knowledge is anything less than that, you stand to lose your affluent prospect's trust.

In Chapter 3, you learned that concept selling is the heart and soul of creating a successful affluent sales environment. As you begin to understand your prospect's goals and aspirations, within the context of your product and service strategy, the exact functional features and pricing become less important. Your knowledge becomes part of the value that your customer buys, and you have established an ongoing relationship. You have become the trusted source of information that will help you pull your affluent prospect closer and closer to the point of sale.

COMMANDMENT 6: PROVIDE VALUE
THAT EXCEEDS PRICE

There's an old saying that *price is only a consideration in the absence of value.* This saying speaks volumes for our sixth affluent commandment. After studying our 2004 APD findings, you might assume that price is not that important to the affluent, especially when it comes to making major purchase decisions. But that is not true. Price is extremely important. These people work hard for their money. But the real issue is not finding the lowest possible price; it's getting the highest possible value for the price that they pay. Although price might appear to be the determining factor in making a major purchase, most of these decisions are determined by a careful examination of the features. Does it have everything I need and want? Is it as advertised? How does it compare to competitive offerings? Price simply needs to be competitive and fair.

There is a tendency for salespeople to remember the prospect who pumped them for information and then went to a competitor for the lowest price. These people are the exception, not the rule. For most affluent buyers, value will include price, but the service factors will carry equal or greater weight. You do not need those "price only" buyers as customers or clients.

Rather than sell on price, make certain that the value you bring to the table exceeds your customers' or clients' expectations. Your role is to clearly articulate that value, and that requires that you master all the other commandments as well.

COMMANDMENT 7: DISCLOSE ALL COSTS

Affluent consumers are a skeptical lot who do not like surprises when making major purchase decisions. That is particularly true if the surprise has a cost hidden somewhere. Just ask any affluent clients what they think about their monthly cell phone bill. Or better yet, how do you like yours? Do you understand it? Have you ever found errors or additional costs that were not explained to you clearly? Have you ever changed carriers because of the surprises? I have, and I'm still not pleased.

Whether it's a hidden service charge on a luxury car that was supposedly under warranty, a rebate that never arrived, or simply fees that were never clearly explained, if you play the unexpected costs game, it will only be a matter of time before you lose a customer or client. This is an extremely important issue with professional services where the fees are often not as clear.

One of the reasons lawyers have become the brunt of so many jokes is their billable hour routine. Although it appears straightforward, few people trust it. The same thing is happening to the financial services industry. Pricing complexity leads to confusion, which then breeds distrust. If you are in the services industry, make certain that your clients have a clear understanding of all fees. When selecting a primary financial coordinator, our 2004 APD Research respondents ranked "clearly revealing their fee structure" as very important in making their decision. You may avoid discussing price with an unsold prospect in order to stay away from selling on price; but at the point of sale, fully disclose all costs. In Chapter 7, we emphasized that there are three things to which your affluent prospect must agree before you can be confident that the sale has been "closed," and one thing is acceptance of the selling price and all associated costs.

COMMANDMENT 8: STAND BY EVERYTHING

In our 2004 APD Research, respondents were given the opportunity to write in other criteria that they considered important when making major purchase decisions. Of all the items listed in that section, one received the greatest attention—the warranty or guarantee. We believe that told us two things. First, it is important that you stand behind everything you sell, clearly stating what you guarantee. Second, it would appear there is some serious dissatisfaction in this area.

Your customers and clients understand that you have little control over corporate policy and that you had nothing to do with creating whatever guarantees and warranties you offer. They also realize that many companies today offer extended warranties to create add-on sales. Your clientele will expect you to know your warranty inside and out; and if there is an extended warranty that can be purchased, they will expect you to do more than simply pressure them to purchase it. Communication and clarity are the issue here. They will want informed assistance in making their decision. Make certain that you spend the time to explain everything carefully and, based on what you have learned about your clientele, provide an honest recommendation regarding options to extend the warranty period. Trust is the critical ingredient for building a long-term relationship.

COMMANDMENT 9: YOU ARE THE FIRM

This is obvious in the world of intangibles. A service provider is the product as far as his or her clients are concerned. But the same holds true with providers of tangible products. When dealing with the affluent, whether you are selling a $25,000 entertainment system, a second home, or a luxury automobile, you are the firm in your customer's or client's mind. That is why in Chapter 9 you are encouraged to accept full personal responsibility for everything that touches your customer or client, which includes getting to know and winning the cooperation of your service department. Like the NFL quarterback who takes his entire offensive line out to dinner after winning the game on Sunday, you need to have service people working with you to achieve the same goals—earning the respect and loyalty of each and every affluent customer and client.

COMMANDMENT 10: BE COVETOUS OF YOUR REPUTATION

Each of these commandments will have a direct impact on your reputation. Commit yourself to them, and your reputation will likely soar. Neglect these commandments, and your reputation will suffer. Because so much of your success in the affluent world involves word-of-mouth influence, whether directly or indirectly, it is important to include reputation as a separate commandment.

When it comes to reputation, everything counts. Every part of every chapter in this book is vital, and it all works together to shape your reputation. It doesn't matter whether you are on the sidelines watching your daughter's soccer team play a weekend match, at a sports bar watching a ballgame, or dealing with a client problem in your office—it all matters. Solving a client problem is obvious. Resolve it quickly and to the client's satisfaction, and it directly impacts repeat business and referrals—unless what he or she sees of you on the soccer field or in the sports bar is inconsistent with the image you attempt to portray at work. As a salesperson who is committed to becoming one with the affluent, you are always "at work."

COMMANDMENT 11: BECOME INTERNET SAVVY

Recently, I received an unsolicited e-mail brochure from a team of financial advisors in Chicago. Since I live in Greensboro, North Carolina, I found it odd that I was receiving a prospecting contact from two people I never met. I knew what they looked like because their picture was on the e-brochure. Because I do a lot of work in the financial services industry, my initial response was one of curiosity. I thought maybe I knew them, but I did not.

Once I got past my curiosity, I realized that this was simply another piece of spam e-mail similar to all the others I receive daily. If they were truly Internet savvy, they would realize that the growing complaints about spam e-mail, the recent CAN-SPAM legislation, and the efforts among Internet service providers to filter and block spam make it prudent to engage only in permission-based e-mail marketing. If you are not certain of what all that means, it is important that you take steps to find out.

You will also want to use the Internet to assist your prospective clients in doing their research. Helping prospects conduct their major purchase due diligence will have a major impact on their decision-making process. That requires that you have a web site, use keywords and phrases to list your web site where prospective buyers will find you, and design your web site to facilitate their efforts to learn about the products and/or services you offer. Remember, the affluent do a lot of prepurchase research, they are Internet savvy, and they use it as their primary prepurchase research vehicle. You will also want to offer free information on your web site that visitors can receive by giving you their name and e-mail address, which is a key aspect of permission-based e-mail marketing.

When you take the step to create your personal online presence, you will move to the head of the class.

COMMANDMENT 12: NO HASSLES

This commandment might appear to be another blinding glimpse of the obvious, and it is. But I cannot emphasize strongly enough the role that stress plays in the life of your affluent clientele. It is huge! Few people who work 60 or more hours a week are low on the stress charts. Few affluent people have the time or patience for unnecessary hassles. You already know the importance that problem solving and first-class service carry when it comes to client loyalty and referrals. What you may not have realized is that your customers and clients want to be loyal because it mitigates the hassles factor. They do not have to spend the time to find another trusted supplier.

What about the hassles involved in dealing with you or your company? Recently, a financial advisor shared his tale of woe with me concerning an affluent prospect who was referred by the prospect's CPA. That was a good start. The financial advisor called, set up an appointment, and asked the prospect to bring all of his financial information to the first meeting. The meeting went well, and the financial advisor scheduled a second meeting for two weeks into the future, at which time he would present a financial plan to his prospective client.

Then the problems began. The financial plans were done by financial planners in a central location, which meant that the advisor had to send all the prospect's information to them. The advisor then discovered that his firm had upgraded their planning software, and the information he sent to the planning department was inadequate. This forced the financial advisor to contact his affluent prospect to pick up some additional papers. Once may not have been so bad, but this happened three separate times and required that the follow-up meeting be postponed. When he called his prospect the third time, the prospect commented, "It just seems like this whole process is too much of a hassle."

Make a list of every prospect and customer or client contact point related to your business—before, during, and after the sale. Beside each contact point, write down anything that typically occurs that might test the patience of a busy, stressed, affluent prospect, customer, or client. You know what to do next: Eliminate those problems so that dealing with you and your firm becomes a truly hassle-free experience.

Eliminate hassles for prospects, and they will become customers and clients. Eliminate hassles for customers and clients, and they will continue to sing your praises and help you on your road to affluence.

As you master these 12 commandments of affluent selling, think of yourself as working on your PhD in affluence. You want to be a lifetime student of the affluent. You want to know their likes, dislikes, pet peeves, how they make buying decisions, what influences them, their ego defenses, how hard they work, the stress in their lives—everything. In many ways, you want to know them better than they know themselves. Refer to these commandments as a reminder. Reread the chapters when you might need a review. But most of all, continually renew your vow to achieve affluence and remain on the parallel paths of mastery of the art of selling to the affluent and acquiring personal affluence.

Appendix

THE 2004 AFFLUENT PURCHASING
DECISION RESEARCH

As the twentieth century came to a close, we conducted an independent study of affluent investors across the United States. Our goal was to uncover what it would take for financial professionals to gain and maintain client loyalty from affluent investors in the twenty-first century. The average yearly income of our respondents was $135,000.

Results from the research were startling, but not unexpected. Survey respondents reported that financial professionals were not meeting their expectations in 14 of the 20 qualities that they rated as being most important. From that research, we initiated an ongoing effort to help financial advisors and wealth management teams improve their performance in attracting, servicing, and retaining the loyalty of affluent investors.

We have continued to conduct research since that time, focusing on varying aspects of the financial services industry. In early 2004, we decided to expand our focus and look at the purchasing decision-making process of the affluent in a wide range of areas. Our stated goal for this survey was to find answers to this question:

> What are the key factors that guide the financial manage-
> ment, normal budget, and major item purchase decisions of
> high-income individuals?

The results of our national 2004 Affluent Purchasing Decision
(APD) Research project are presented here. The survey was conducted for the Oechsli Institute of Greensboro, North Carolina, by
Jacokes & Associates of Grand Rapids, Michigan, during May and
June 2004. A random sample of 400 men and women with household incomes of $100,000 or greater was surveyed. The sample was
drawn from households across the United States. Four hundred respondents completed the survey, providing us a ±4.8 percent error
rate at a 95 percent confidence level. Following are several of the
more significant findings of the research:

- The sample of 400 respondents presents a reasonable rep-
  resentation of age, household income, and geographic
  characteristics.
- Of the respondents, 92.3 percent generate their own wealth.
  They include business owners, self-employed professionals,
  corporate executives, and commissioned employees (salespeople).
- Respondents were asked to evaluate *10 criteria* related to
  selecting a primary banking service. The responses were
  analyzed from two perspectives—the importance to the respondents and the performance of the respondents' current
  primary bank. The gap between expectations and performance was also calculated. We discovered the following:
  —The two criteria rated as the most important in selecting a
  primary bank were having a reputation for high-quality
  service and having convenient branch and ATM locations.
  The gaps between expectations and performance for both
  criteria were high.

—Providing personalized services fell in the middle in terms of importance, but the gap between expectations and performance in this area was also high.

—The criteria rated least important were offering investment products of varying risks and maturities and assisting with business-related areas. There were no gaps between expectations and performance in these areas.

- The research indicates that banks have not yet positioned themselves effectively in the investment advisory role, and it's clear that much of what banks do offer is viewed primarily as a commodity. Looking at the areas with the strongest gaps between expectations and performance suggests that banks need to strengthen their advisory role, not only in investments but also in all financial service areas. Even though close to 50 percent of the respondents were self-employed, only 20.4 percent said that having their bank assist them with cash management needs was very important.

- Respondents were asked who they use as a provider of financial products and services. Their choices were CPA, financial planner, financial advisor, personal banker, and attorney. The most used is a CPA; the least used are personal bankers and attorneys.

- *Eight qualities* associated with selecting a primary financial coordinator were also analyzed from two perspectives: the importance to the respondents and the performance of the respondents' financial professionals. Gaps between the respondents' expectations and the performance of their current financial coordinators were also calculated. We discovered the following:

    —The qualities rated as most important were clearly understanding the respondents' goals and family situation when giving investment advice, clearly revealing the advisor's fee structure, and being proactive in contacting and coordinating upcoming tax and other changes that will impact their investment portfolio. There were serious gaps between expectations and performance in all three areas.

—All eight qualities were rated as very important by at least 42 percent of the respondents, and there were significant gaps between expectations and performance in all eight areas.

—When it comes to managing their financial affairs, the affluent are having difficulty finding a trusted go-to financial coordinator to oversee all of their financial affairs. Having their assets managed by two or three different advisors means no one is taking an integrated approach that minimizes taxes, maximizes growth opportunities, and ensures asset protection in tough times.

- *Seven qualities* associated with making major purchase decisions were analyzed in terms of importance to the respondents. Here is what we found:

—Two criteria stood above the rest: 83.3 percent said that offering the right set of features was very important; 75.8 percent said that being able to find the best possible option through careful evaluation and comparison was very important.

—65.5 percent said that the opinions of immediate family members and trusted friends had very significant impact on deciding where to look when making a major purchase decision, but only 37.8 percent said those opinions have a very significant impact on their final purchase decision.

—Once the search process is underway, the affluent place more confidence in their own ability to find the information they need, sort through the options, and make the final decision. Respondents also indicated that the Internet and trusted periodicals serve as their major research vehicles.

—When given an opportunity to write in other criteria considered important when making major purchase decisions, warranty and guarantee were the most frequently stated by a wide margin.

—Even though respondents were extremely price-value conscious, finding a discounted or a sale price was not as critical to their final major purchase decision as we expected it would be.

- *Seven factors* were used to determine what influenced the respondents to use the same major product or service provider again. Problem resolution and postpurchase service rated as having the greatest impact on repeat business. Offering the lowest price ranked last.

- *Five criteria* were used to probe respondents' decision making regarding normal budget purchase decisions for home, business, medical, entertainment, and education. Looking across all five criteria, respondents were consistently concerned about the total cost being within their budget. Value was also a key issue. Respondents gave far less importance to reviews and testimonials than they did to the responsiveness of sales and service people.

DEMOGRAPHICS

Survey respondents were screened to ensure that everyone taking the survey had a personal income of $100,000 or higher. The specific demographics include the following:

Breakdown of Personal Income Level

$1 million or higher	1.9 percent
$500,000 to $999,000	2.3 percent
$250,000 to $499,000	13.0 percent
$100,000 to $249,000	82.8 percent

Primary Source of Personal Annual Income

Result of ownership	22.4 percent
Self-employed professional	25.9 percent
Salary and commission	44.9 percent
Retirement	2.7 percent
Inheritance	0.6 percent
Other	3.5 percent

Percent of Household Income That the Respondent Provides

80 percent or higher	50.5 percent
70 percent to under 80 percent	12.4 percent
60 percent to under 70 percent	14.5 percent
50 percent to under 60 percent	12.2 percent
Under 50 percent	10.4 percent

Number of Hours per Week Spent Working in Their Occupation

Over 60 hours	25.9 percent
50 to 60 hours	32.3 percent
40 to 50 hours	24.4 percent
40 hours or less	17.4 percent

Gender

Male	82.2 percent
Female	17.8 percent

Age

Over 65	7.1 percent
50 to 64	42.9 percent
35 to 49	39.0 percent
Under 35	11.0 percent

Highest Level of Education

Graduate level, college	41.7 percent
Undergrad, college	38.8 percent
High school	17.8 percent
Not completed high school	1.7 percent

Primary Residence Location

New England	6.2 percent
Mid-Atlantic	23.9 percent
South	19.7 percent
Midwest	28.4 percent
Southwest	7.7 percent
West	13.5 percent
Other	0.6 percent

Marital Status

Single	10.4 percent
Married, no children	11.5 percent
Married, child at home	39.6 percent
Married, children not at home	32.6 percent
Divorced, not married	4.4 percent
Widowed, not married	1.5 percent

FINANCIAL DECISION MAKING

Financial decision making focused on two areas: selecting a primary banking service and selecting a primary financial coordinator:

1. *Selecting a primary banking service:* Following is the list of selection criteria that respondents said were important to them—along with the percent reporting each criterion as *very important:*
   - Has a reputation for high-quality service—74.8 percent
   - Has convenient branch and ATM locations—63.8 percent

- Charges the lowest possible product and service costs— 60.1 percent
- Will provide Internet banking services—50.9 percent
- Will assist with qualifying for the loan option that best meets my needs—37.9 percent
- Will provide 24-hour private banking services—32 percent
- Will provide a personal banking representative—28.7 percent
- Offers investment products of varying risks and maturities—15.1 percent

The following relate specifically to business owners:

- Will assist with cash management needs for my business— 20.4 percent
- Will assist with finding financial information about my industry—11.2 percent

The first six items also showed statistically significant gaps between respondent expectations and the performance of their current bank. From the regression analysis of the performance scores, four criteria emerged as being the most important in explaining variances in overall bank performance:

- Having a reputation for high-quality performance
- Will assist you with qualifying for the loan option that best meets your needs
- Will provide a personal banking representative
- Offers investment products of varying risks and maturities

Efforts to improve and promote these four areas should provide a good return on that investment of effort.

2. *Selecting a primary financial coordinator:* Following is the list of selection criteria that respondents said were important to them—along with the percent reporting each criterion as *very important:*
   - Clearly understands your goals and family situation when giving investment advice—78.8 percent
   - Clearly reveals their fee structure—70.8 percent

- Is proactive about contacting you when upcoming tax and other changes will impact your investment portfolio—69.8 percent
- Helps you create a formal financial plan—59.0 percent
- Helps you select the asset mix for your investment portfolio—57.5 percent
- Helps you coordinate and organize all financial documents—47.6 percent
- Coordinates investment decisions—46.7 percent
- Brings in experts to help with other financial areas—42.0 percent

All eight items showed statistically significant gaps between respondent expectations and the performance of their current financial coordinator. From the regression analysis of the performance scores, three criteria emerged as being the most important in explaining variances in overall bank performance:

- Clearly reveals their fee structure
- Helps coordinate and organize all financial documents
- Brings in experts to help with other financial areas

Efforts to improve and promote these three areas should provide a good return on that investment. However, the fact that significant performance gaps exist in all eight criteria suggests that a serious overall performance challenge exists.

NORMAL BUDGET PURCHASE DECISIONS

This was defined as products and services that the respondents purchase from their annual income without having to borrow money or use credit cards to finance the purchase beyond 90 days. Normal budget categories included choice of products and services for home use, choice of products and services for business use, choice of medical and health services, choice of entertainment provided outside the home, and choice of formal education institutions and programs.

1. *Choice of products and services for home use:* Following is the list of selection criteria that respondents said were important to them—along with the percent reporting each criterion as *very important:*
   - Offers the right set of features—73 percent
   - Total cost is within our budget—65 percent
   - Finding the best possible option through careful evaluation and comparison—64.7 percent
   - Responsiveness of sales and service people—55.7 percent
   - Finding a discounted or sales price—36.7 percent
   - What reviews, testimonials, and other sources say about the product or service quality—36.7 percent

2. *Choice of products and services for business use:* Following is the list of selection criteria that respondents said were important to them—along with the percent reporting each criterion as *very important:*
   - Offers the right set of features—77.1 percent
   - Total cost is within our budget—71.3 percent
   - Finding the best possible option through careful evaluation and comparison—70.1 percent
   - Responsiveness of sales and service people—61.3 percent
   - What reviews, testimonials, and other sources say about the product or service quality—40.9 percent
   - Finding a discounted or sales price—39.2 percent

   Even though the percentages were slightly different, it's clear that the priority of selection criteria is the same for home and business use products and services.

3. *Choice of medical and health services for themselves and their family:* Following is the list of selection criteria that respondents said were important to them—along with the percent reporting each criterion as *very important:*
   - Whether the provider and service is covered by our insurance—65.2 percent
   - What other sources say about the competence of the providers—56.4 percent

- The total cost is within our budget—53.8 percent
- What other sources say about the services provided—52.6 percent
- Convenience of things such as distance and easy access—49.4 percent

4. *Choice of entertainment provided outside the home:* Following is the list of selection criteria that respondents said were important to them—along with the percent reporting each criterion as *very important:*
   - It is something we very much wanted to see and experience—71.5 percent
   - The total cost is within our budget—54 percent
   - We felt it was the best entertainment option available at that time—40.1 percent
   - Convenience of things such as distance, parking, and ease of obtaining tickets—33.3 percent
   - What reviews, testimonies, and other sources say about the quality of that entertainment—29.7 percent
   - Finding a discounted or sales price—26.3 percent

5. *Choice of formal education institutions and programs to be attended by yourself and your immediate family:* Following is the list of selection criteria that respondents said were important to them—along with the percent reporting each criterion as *very important:*
   - Being convinced that the specific course/degree is an important investment for the future—69.3 percent
   - I/we felt it was the best possible educational option available at that time—66.9 percent
   - The cost is within our budget—49.1 percent
   - What reviews, testimonials, and other sources say about the quality of the education/degrees offered—45.3 percent
   - Convenience of things such as distance, parking, and assistance with selection and registration—24.6 percent
   - Finding a reasonable or discounted price—22.4 percent

MAJOR PURCHASE DECISIONS

This was defined as products and services that meet all of the following criteria:

- The product or service will last over a year (e.g., car, boat, appliance) . . . or an antique or fine art they admire and believe has investment value (e.g., painting, sculpture, antique furniture) . . . or is a one-time special event or activity (e.g., dream vacation, daughter's wedding, large Christmas party).
- The cost is high enough to require financing outside their normal budget.
- The cost is high enough that they believe the purchase decision requires careful analysis.

The total amount that respondents and their immediate family spent on major purchases over the past 12 months was broken down as follows:

$100,000 or higher	8.8 percent
$50,000 to $99,999	14.3 percent
$25,000 to $49,000	26.0 percent
$10,000 to $24,999	24.5 percent
$5,000 to $9,999	13.0 percent
$1,000 to $4,999	10.4 percent
Under $1,000	3.0 percent

The major purchase decision process was evaluated in three stages: deciding where to look for options, making the purchase decision, and deciding whether to use the same product or service provider again:

- *Deciding where to look for major purchase options:* Following is a list of criteria they used to make that selection, with the percent who said they gave *considerable credibility* to that particular criterion:

—Opinions and suggestions of my immediate family—
34.8 percent

—Opinions and suggestions of trusted friends—30.8 percent

—Information I find in specific periodicals—25.5 percent

—Information I find on the Internet—15.8 percent

—The advice and recommendations of salespeople—
2.5 percent

- *Making the purchase decision:* Following is a list of criteria respondents used to make that decision, with the percent who said each criterion was *very important:*

—It offers the right set of features—83.3 percent

—Finding the best possible option through careful evaluation and comparison—75.8 percent

—Finding a discounted or sale price—39.8 percent

—Responsiveness of sales and service people—37.5 percent

—What reviews, testimonials, and other sources say about product and service quality—37.0 percent

—The opinions of my immediate family—23 percent

—The opinions of trusted friends—14.8 percent

Respondents were also given an opportunity to write in other criteria they considered important when making the final decision. The one item that appeared numerous times was warranty and warranty period.

- *Deciding whether to use the same product or service provider again:* Following is a list of criteria they used to make that decision, with the percent who said that particular criterion had *considerable influence* on that decision:

—Any problems I encountered were resolved quickly and satisfactorily—90.3 percent

—They provided good service following my purchase—
81.8 percent

—They provided the information I needed to make a satisfactory purchase decision—69.5 percent

—Their guarantees of satisfaction were clearly defined—
65.8 percent
—The brand I prefer is available through them—63.0 percent
—The people who represented them were friendly and help-
ful—62.5 percent
—They offered the lowest price available—44.3 percent

Breaking the major purchase decision into three phases enabled us to apply this research specifically to the prospecting, sales, and postsale dimensions of this book. This was important because it is clear that different influences take over as the affluent move from one phase of their decision-making process to another.

REFERENCES

American Express/Roper ASW Global Affluent Study. London: Roper ASW.

Belluck, Pam. "Doctors' New Deluxe Practices Offer Deluxe Service for Deluxe Fee." *New York Times* (January 15, 2002).

Cap Gemini Ernst & Young. *Wealth Management Strategies for the Financial Services Industry* (White paper). August 22, 2002.

Carnegie, Dale. *How to Win Friends and Influence People.* New York: Pocket Books, 1990.

Covey, Stephen. *First Things First.* New York: Free Press, 1996, p. 384.

Dudley, George W., and Shannon L. Goodson. *The Psychology of Sales Call Reluctance: Earning What You're Worth.* Dallas, TX: Behavioral Sciences Research Press, Inc., 1999.

Gottlieb, Dan. "At Home, School, Give Kids a Stress Break." *Philadelphia Inquirer* (September 20, 2004).

Helmstetter, Shad. *The Self-Talk Solution.* New York: Pocket Books, 1988, p. 14.

Livingston, J. Sterling. "Pygmalion in Management." *Harvard Business Review* (January 2003, p. 97).

Molloy, John T. *New Dress for Success.* New York: Warner Books, 1998.

Molloy, John T. *New Women's Dress for Success.* New York: Warner Books, 1996.

Morrissey, Briar, "Defining Dayparts," Click.com news (washingtonpost.com and Nielsen Ratings research, February 6, 2003).

NFO WorldGroup. "Millionaire Investors Go Solo: Financial Advisors Receive a 'C' " Grade for Competence and Confidence." Affluent Market Research Program, October 30, 2002.

Oechsli, Matt. *Mastering High Net Worth Selling.* Greensboro, NC: Total Achievement Publishing, 2003.

Oechsli Institute. *Clients' Perceptions of Financial Professionals* (Research report). Grand Rapids, MI: Jacokes & Associates, 1999.

Outward Insights. *Attracting and Retaining Affluent Customers: Selected Best Practices for Financial Services Institutions* (Research report). 2003.

Plimpton, George. Interview with TIME.com, American Online Transcript (June 14, 1999).

Plimpton, George, *Paper Lion: Confession of a Last String Quarterback* Guilford, CT: Lyons Press, 2003.

Popek, Joan. "Roswell, New Mexico: The City with a Magnetic Personality." SouthernNewMexico.com (January 23, 2003).

Prince, Russ A., and Karen Maru File. *Cultivating the Affluent II: Leveraging High-Net-Worth Client and Advisor Relationships.* New York: Institutional Investor, 1997.

Punishill, Jamie, with Bill Doyle and Tom Watson. "How Affluent Investors Use the Internet: A Look at Millionaires and Their Money from 1998 to Today." Forrester.com (March 31, 2004).

Ritz-Carlton. *Credo.* The Ritz-Carlton Basics: Three Steps of Service.

Stanely, Thomas J., and William D. Danko, *The Millionaire Next Door.* New York: Pocket Books, 1998.

Weyner, Alison Stein. "The Income Report." *American Demographics* magazine, (December 2002).

INDEX

ABOUT THE AUTHOR

M att Oechsli is the founder and president of the Oechsli Institute, an internationally recognized consulting and research
firm with clients such as American Express, Merrill Lynch, Wa-
chovia, Morgan Stanley, and Pioneer Investments. He is a leading
authority and much sought-after speaker on how to attract, service,
and retain affluent customers and clients.